Progress Monitoring
Assessments

PEARSON

Prentice
Hall

Boston, Massachusetts
Upper Saddle River, New Jersey

Credits: Pages 96 and 117: "Using NASA Technology" adapted from an article published by *NASA Explores*, May 1, 2001, **http://www.nasaexplores.com/lessons/01-038/5-8_index.html**

Pearson Prentice Hall™ is a trademark of Pearson Education, Inc.
Pearson® is a registered trademark of Pearson plc.
Prentice Hall® is a registered trademark of Pearson Education, Inc.

ISBN 0-13-190167-2
5 6 7 8 9 10   10 09 08 07 06

TABLE OF CONTENTS

TABLE OF CONTENTS

Since state assessments must be aligned with state curriculum standards as part of the *No Child Left Behind Act of 2001 (NCLB)*, administering tests on a regular basis will allow you to monitor your students' proficiency levels. To be sure that all students will achieve success, students' performances on these tests should be linked to review and practice activities.

How to Use This Workbook

Progress Monitoring Assessments provides a clear path to *adequate yearly progress* through systematic testing and recommendations for remediation. Progress monitoring at regular intervals ensures that students understand key content before moving on in the course. With the results of these tests, you will know when to modify instruction because a class is having difficulty and when to assign remediation because individual students need more help.

Beginning the Year: Establishing the Baseline

Teaching for adequate yearly progress begins with evaluating student strengths and weaknesses. Before launching into the curriculum, you need to know how proficient your students are in science process and basic math skills as well as their background knowledge in science concepts. Use the following tests to measure student readiness for your course.

Screening Tests

Administer the *Screening Tests* to evaluate students' understanding of science process and basic math skills. You may wish to consider placing students who do not perform well on this test in intensive intervention. For students who have less difficulty, you can use the recommendations for differentiated instruction in the Teacher's Edition of your textbook.

Diagnostic Tests

The *Diagnostic Tests* help you identify areas in which individual students are having difficulty. After students have taken the tests, complete a *Diagnostic Report* for each student. The reports will help you pinpoint which standards students know and where weaknesses exist. Determine what is an acceptable level of proficiency for your students.

The *Diagnostic Report* can be shared with students and parents. At the end of the report is a place for a parent signature if you choose to use the report as part of your communication plan with parents.

Standardized Test Preparation Workbook Answer Key and Correlations

The *SAT9, ITBS, TerraNova,* and *NAEP* tests in the *Standardized Test Preparation Workbook* give students practice taking tests to improve their scores on standardized tests. Each question in the Diagnostic Tests, Grade 6, 7, and 8 is correlated to SAT9, ITBS, and TerraNova science objectives. The Practice Test answers and correlations are included in this book.

Monitoring Progress Over the Year

The section and chapter assessments in the Student Edition and All-in-One Teaching Resources measure understanding of what students have learned on a short-term basis. To measure student retention over time, it is important to administer tests and refocus instruction based on test results.

Ending the Year

Modifying your teaching as indicated by the results of the Screening and Diagnostic Tests sets the stage for your students to achieve adequate yearly progress.

Correlating Test Questions

For the test contained in this workbook, there are comprehensive test reports that provide valuable information for you and your students. Each diagnostic test item is referenced to an SAT9, ITBS, and TerraNova Test, and to the Science Objectives. Below is an example of one of the reports.

TESTS			Earth Science Objectives	Question Numbers Test A	Question Numbers Test B	Number Correct	Proficient? Yes or No
SAT9	ITBS	TerraNova					
Topic: Scientific Inquiry/Processes							
	✓	✓	1 Understand the fundamental concepts of science inquiry.	1, 2, 3	29, 30, 31		
✓	✓		2 Demonstrate the ability to perform science inquiry.	4, 5, 6	23, 24, 25		
✓	✓		3 Use the process skills of science. • Draw a conclusion from data. • Evaluate graphs of experimental data.	7, 8, 9	9, 10, 11		
	✓		4 Apply safety skills.	10, 11, 12	38, 39, 40		
	✓		5 Understand, use, and convert SI units.	13, 14, 15	32, 33, 34		
Topic: History and Nature of Science							
		✓	1 Understand science as a human endeavor. • Understand the changing nature of scientific knowledge. • Understand the history of science.	16, 17, 18	26, 27, 28		
Topic: Earth's Water							
✓		✓	1 Describe the water cycle. • Identify parts of the water cycle. • Describe the distribution of fresh water and salt water on Earth.	19, 20, 21 22, 23	12, 13, 14, 15, 16		
✓			2 Describe the characteristics of Earth's oceans. • Recognize the chemical and physical properties of ocean water. • Discuss the movements of ocean water in currents, tides, and waves. • Interpret a profile of the ocean floor.	24, 25, 26, 27, 28, 29, 30, 31	1, 2, 3, 4, 5, 6, 7, 8		
		✓	3 Describe ocean life. • Recognize the different life zones in the ocean. • Identify three groups of ocean life.	32, 33, 34	35, 36, 37		

SCREENING TEST, Part 1, BASIC PROCESS SKILLS

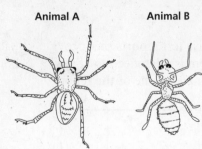

Animal A **Animal B**

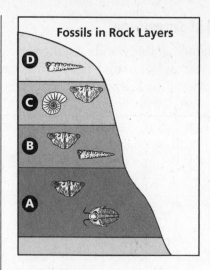

Fossils in Rock Layers

1. Which of the following statements is a quantitative observation you can make about the animals shown in the diagram above?

   A Both animals are invertebrates that live on land.

   B Animal A has a narrow body with a pattern on its back and extremely long legs.

   C Animal B has a body with three main sections, two antennae on its head, and three pairs of legs.

   D Both animals have a similar appearance, but Animal A appears bigger than Animal B.

2. Insects are animals that have three main body parts and six legs. Given that information, how would you classify the animals in the diagram above?

   A Both animals are insects.

   B Animal A is an insect, but Animal B is not.

   C Animal B is an insect, but Animal A is not.

   D Neither animal is an insect.

3. The diagram shows a sketch of fossils, or preserved remains, found at different rock layers at a particular location. Which of the following statements is a qualitative observation based on this diagram?

   A The four types of fossils are classified as different kinds of animals.

   B The fossils in layer A are ancestors of the fossils in other layers.

   C The bottom fossil in layer A has a body that is made up of segments.

   D Scientists can use this diagram to help learn how old each fossil is.

4. A corn seed is shaped something like a pizza slice. No matter how corn seeds are positioned in the soil, however, the roots always grow downward, and the stems always grow upward. Which of the following is the most logical inference for this pattern?

   A The seeds are responding to the touch of the surrounding soil.

   B The seeds are responding to the chemicals in the leaves and flowers.

   C The seeds are responding to the sunlight.

   D The seeds are responding to gravity.

SCREENING TEST, Part 1 *(continued)*

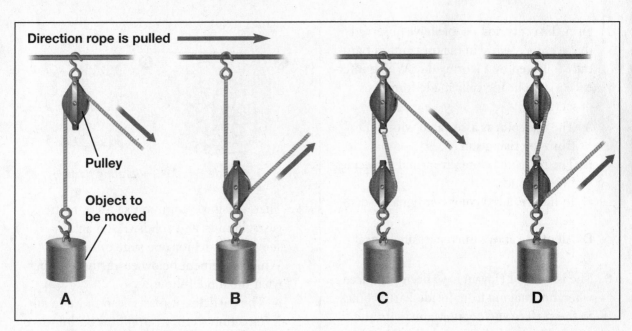

Direction rope is pulled

Pulley

Object to be moved

A   B   C   D

5. Pulleys are one type of simple machine. A pulley is a grooved wheel with a rope or cable wrapped around it. Which statement is an accurate observation about the pulleys shown in the diagram?

A The diagram shows four different kinds of simple machines, which can be combined in various ways.

B All the ropes should be pulled in the same direction when the pulleys are used.

C Two machines are made up of single pulleys, while the other machines are made up of two pulleys.

D Pulleys make work easier by allowing you to change the amount or direction of the force you exert.

6. Which statement is a logical inference based on the pulleys diagrammed above?

A If you pull on each of the ropes, the objects will be lifted upward.

B If you pull on the rope in pulley B, the object will be lowered.

C Because pulley system C has two pulleys, you will need two people to pull on the rope to move the object.

D You need to see more of the ropes before you can make inferences about the pulleys.

SCREENING TEST, Part 1 *(continued)*

7. Over the centuries, people have observed that a red sky early in the morning is typically followed by a stormy day. Which inference(s) can be logically made from that observation?

   A The red color is associated with light from the rising sun.

   B The red color comes from red molecules in the clouds.

   C In nature, a red color is a signal of danger.

   D All of the above inferences are logical.

8. The islands of Hawaii have been produced when hot magma from inside Earth comes to the surface and cools. Many years after it erupts, the hardened magma becomes home to plants, animals, and other living things. Which of the following is the most logical prediction about newly erupted magma?

   A More magma will erupt in the future, increasing the total area of the islands.

   B People will need to establish farms and villages to make the newly cooled magma useful.

   C In the past, living things always moved in to live on the cooled magma.

   D Although the cooled magma has no life on it at first, it will eventually support a variety of living things.

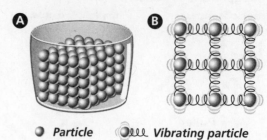

● *Particle* ◖◗◖◗◖◗ *Vibrating particle*

9. There are three common states of matter: gases, liquids, and solids. The diagram shows a model for one state of matter. Which statement below correctly describes what the model shows?

   A The particles of matter can move in any direction so they can fill the entire space of their container.

   B The particles of matter are completely free to move, so the matter takes on the shape of its container.

   C The particles can vibrate, but they stay in fixed positions, causing the matter to have a definite shape and volume.

   D The particles cause the matter to have a fixed shape because they have no energy related to motion.

SCREENING TEST, Part 1 *(continued)*

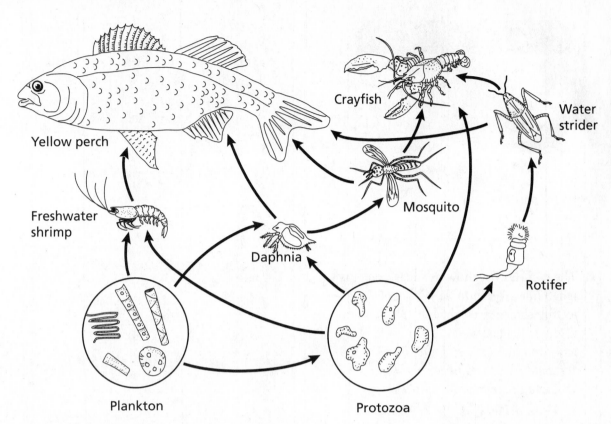

10. The diagram shows a model of a freshwater food web. Which statement correctly describes what the model shows?

A The food web shows all the things that live in or near a freshwater pond.

B Decomposers are not needed in this food web.

C The arrows flow from the living thing that is eaten to the living thing(s) that eat it.

D The model is a three-dimensional model because it shows producers, first-level consumers, and higher-level consumers.

SCREENING TEST, Part 1 *(continued)*

Title?	
Temperature (°C)	Speed of Sound (m/s)
0	331
15	340
20	344
30	349
40	354
50	360
100	386

11. The table above, showing measurements made in air, has no title. Which of the following choices would be the most useful title for this table?

   A Speed of Sound in Different Materials
   B Speed of Sound in Air
   C Changing Air Temperatures
   D Differences in Sound Waves

12. In the table above, examine the two columns of data about temperature and speed of sound in air. Which of the following is the most accurate prediction that can be made based on that data?

   A Below 0°C, the speed of sound in air will be constant.
   B At 30°C, the speed of sound will be about 350 m/s.
   C At 120°C, the speed of sound will be about 360 m/s.
   D The lower the air temperature, the faster the speed of sound will be.

13. More than 80 metals are found in nature. Metals can be classified by their atomic structure. The diagrams of six metals show their valence electrons, the electrons farther from the nucleus. Based on the structures shown, which way of classifying the metals would be the most useful?

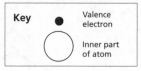

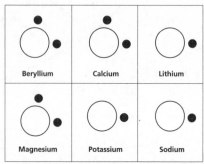

   A Use 6 groups, one group per metal.
   B Use 1 group containing six metals.
   C Use 2 groups, one having a single valence electron, and the other having two valence electrons.
   D Use 3 groups: metals, nonmentals, and metalloids.

14. Suppose your class is creating your own system for classifying rocks. You plan to share the classification system with students in other parts of the world and compare rocks from different locations. Which guideline should be the most important as you create the new system?

   A Include all the known scientific and technical names for rocks.
   B Create a system that will work for all kinds of rocks.
   C Be sure the system makes it easy to store the rocks you collect.
   D Focus on the rocks that are frequently found in your community.

SCREENING TEST, Part 1 *(continued)*

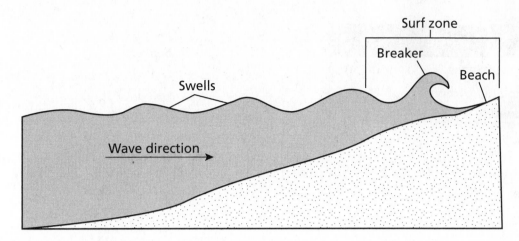

15. The diagram above shows a two-dimensional model of ocean waves. What would indicate whether this model is drawn to scale?

   A Whether it is the same size as the real objects it shows

   B Whether it contains measurements in the metric system

   C Whether its measurements are in the same proportions as the actual objects

   D Whether it is smaller or larger than the real objects

Thermometer Readings (°C)

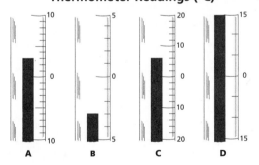

16. Which thermometer reading in the diagram correctly shows a reading of 3°C?

   A Thermometer A

   B Thermometer B

   C Thermometer C

   D Thermometer D

17. Suppose you heard a person make this prediction: "There will be a major rain storm next weekend." What would be the best reason for saying that the prediction was scientific?

   A The person made the prediction during a televised weather report.

   B The person making the prediction gave numerous details about winds and temperatures.

   C The person based the prediction on a body of evidence.

   D The prediction is an inference, not a fact.

SCREENING TEST, Part 1 *(continued)*

Title?	
Type of Snake	**Length (m)**
Reticulated python	8
Anaconda	5
Mamba	3.5
King cobra	3.4
Boa constrictor	3.3
Eastern rattlesnake	2.5
Grass snake	1

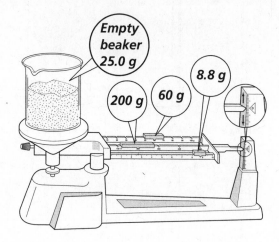

18. Examine the table of data above. Which of the following choices would be the best title for the table?

A Length of Different Kinds of Snakes
B Types of Snakes
C Length (m)
D How Snakes Differ

19. Examine the data in the table above. Would it be useful to show these data in a circle graph?

A Yes, because the snake lengths make up the parts of a whole
B Yes, because the graph will then show which percent each type of snake represents
C No, because the snake lengths do not make up the parts of a whole
D No, because the data are made up of averages, and they should be on a line graph

20. Which statement below accurately describes the mass of the solid in the diagram above?

A 268.89
B 200 g
C 243.8 g
D There is no way to find the mass of the solid using this information.

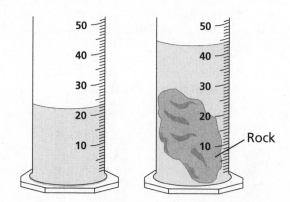

21. The diagram above shows one way to measure the volume of an irregular object. Which of the following measurements gives the correct volume of the rock?

A 43 mL
B 29 mL
C 14 mL
D 21 mL

SCREENING TEST, Part 1 *(continued)*

Household Water Usage	
Activity	**Water Used (L)**
Taking shower	50–77
Taking bath	96–116
Washing hands	4–8
Flushing toilet	19–27
Brushing teeth	19–39
Washing dishes by hand	20–77
Automatic dishwasher	27–58

22. The table above shows the results of a survey of home water usage. You are asked to reorganize the data so that they are easier to understand. Which would be the best way to change the table?

A There is no better way to arrange the information.

B Reorganize the activities in order of the amount of water usage, highest to lowest.

C Retitle the table "What You Need to Know about Water Usage."

D Alphabetize the activities.

23. Which type of graph would best display the data in the table above?

A A bar graph, because the data are made of separate but related categories

B A bar graph, because that graph will show percentages

C A line graph, because differences in the responding variable (water usage) depend on differences in the type of activity

D A line graph, because you can make inferences about values that lie between those that were measured

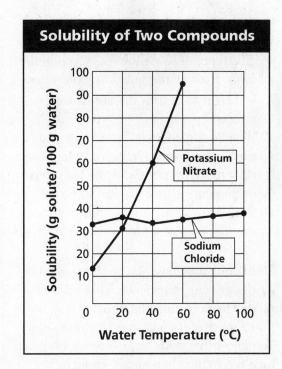

24. The graph shows information about the solubility of two compounds, potassium nitrate and sodium chloride. What does the graph show?

A All substances dissolve in water, but the rates of dissolving are different.

B At 50°C, more grams of potassium nitrate will dissolve than of sodium chloride.

C At 50°C, more grams of sodium chloride will dissolve than of potassium nitrate.

D The cooler the water, the greater the mass of the substance that dissolves.

SCREENING TEST, Part 2, INTEGRATED PROCESS SKILLS

1. Viruses are particles smaller than bacteria. Viruses can cause disease when they invade specific types of living things. Which of the following is a scientific question about viruses?

   A Is it right to destroy disease-causing viruses?

   B Why do some viruses infect only plants, while other viruses infect only animals?

   C How much money should be spent trying to eliminate diseases caused by viruses?

   D Should government make rules for the way diseases caused by viruses are treated?

2. One sunny morning, you see blue morning glories growing on a fence. That night, it rains. The next morning, the flowers are pink, but they soon change to blue again. You know that acids make blue litmus paper turn red. Which hypothesis would be the most logical for explaining why the flower color changed?

   A The growing plant produces acid that causes the flower color to change.

   B The color change occurs when the plants do not get enough water.

   C The color change is caused by acid that is present in the rain.

   D The color change is caused by plant chemicals that break down as the plant grows older.

3. A lab group is choosing a scientific question to research on the Internet. The group chooses to research this question: "What kind of sounds make the best music?" Which of the following statements most correctly describes the group's question?

   A The question is scientific because it can be answered by gathering evidence about the natural world.

   B The question is scientific because the study of sound is a scientific topic.

   C The question is not scientific because it is too broad.

   D The question is not scientific because it involves personal opinions.

Questions About the Sun

a. What materials are present in the sun?

b. How much money can we save by using solar energy?

c. What is the distance between the Earth and the sun?

d. Will the sun ever run out of energy?

---

4. Read the four questions about the sun listed above. Which of those questions are scientific questions?

   A All four questions

   B Only questions "a" and "c"

   C Only questions "b" and "d"

   D Only questions "a," "c," and "d"

5. Your class is investigating metals. You are responsible for designing an experiment to determine which metal is the hardest. All the lab groups will use your plan to investigate different metals, and then the class will combine all the results. Which statement describes the most important part of your job?

   A You need to make sure each lab group collects the same data and reaches the same conclusion.

   B You need to plan a single procedure for all groups to follow, and you need to write an operational definition for hardness.

   C You need to create the same data tables and graphs for all the groups so that they can easily compare their results.

   D You need to get the class to write as many scientific questions about metals as possible, and then eliminate the questions that cannot be answered by gathering evidence.

SCREENING TEST, Part 2 *(continued)*

Operational Definition of Monocot and Dicot		
Procedure	Monocot	Dicot
Examine the veins in the leaf.	parallel veins	branching veins
Cut the stem and examine the vascular tissue.	bundles of vascular tissue scattered throughout the stem	bundles of vascular tissues arranged in ring
Count the flower parts, such as the petals and sepals.	flower parts are in threes	flower parts are in fours or fives

6. Seed plants can be classified as either mono-cots or dicots. The information above can be considered an operational definition of "monocot" and "dicot" because

A it makes a prediction about future events.

B it gives a possible explanation for a set of observations.

C it tells a researcher how to identify monocot and dicot plants.

D it sums up what was learned in an experiment.

7. Rocks at Earth's surface can be broken down by various processes. Which of the following describes a testable hypothesis for investigating this topic?

A Rocks at Earth's surface can be broken down by moving water.

B New rock can be formed when the heat of Earth's interior melts older rocks inside Earth.

C Important historical stone monuments should be protected from weathering.

D Ancient rocks were broken down by so many different processes that we cannot carry out investigations of this topic.

8. Heat is the movement of thermal energy from a warmer substance to a cooler substance. Which of the following statements is a testable hypothesis for investigating whether heat has been transferred?

A If heat is transferred, one material will decrease in temperature, and another material will increase in temperature.

B Temperature measures the average kinetic energy of the particles in a material, so you need to record the temperature of all materials you study.

C Heat can be transferred by the movements of currents in a fluid, as when water in a pot boils.

D If heat has been transferred, good conductors such as metals or floor tiles must be involved, and they will show a change of temperature.

9. Suppose you are planning an experiment to determine which disinfectant is best for killing bacteria often found in kitchens. Which of the following would be the most logical responding variable for your experiment?

A Number of bacteria that survive after using the detergent

B Amount of detergent

C Type of detergent

D Source of bacteria

SCREENING TEST, Part 2 *(continued)*

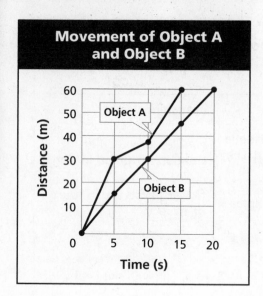

Movement of Object A and Object B

Finding the Hardest Mineral

To determine which of a group of minerals is the hardest, use each mineral to make a scratch on the other minerals. The mineral that can make a scratch on all the other minerals without being scratched itself is the hardest.

10. What information does the graph above explicitly provide?

   A The data points give the speed of the objects at specific times.

   B The graph shows where the objects will be at 25 and 30 seconds.

   C The data points tell how far the objects have moved from the starting points at specific times.

   D The graph shows that one object had to be pushed, while the other object moved on its own.

11. Which statement accurately summarizes what was learned from the graph above?

   A Objects A and B moved in the same direction.

   B Object A moved at a constant speed. Object B's speed changed as it moved.

   C Object A moved faster than Object B.

   D Statements A, B, and C are all accurate.

12. The procedure described above is an example of a(n)

   A controlled variable.

   B manipulated variable.

   C operational definition.

   D scientific prediction.

Identifying an Acid

To find out whether an unknown liquid is an acid, place a drop of the liquid on blue litmus paper. If the litmus paper turns red, the unknown liquid is an acid.

13. Which statement describes whether the directions above provide an operational definition of an acid?

   A The directions are not an operational definition because they do not control the necessary variables.

   B The directions are not an operational definition because they are not clear enough for another person to follow.

   C The directions do provide an operational definition because they clearly tell a researcher how to identify an acid.

   D The directions do provide an operational definition because they avoid opinions and values.

SCREENING TEST, Part 2 *(continued)*

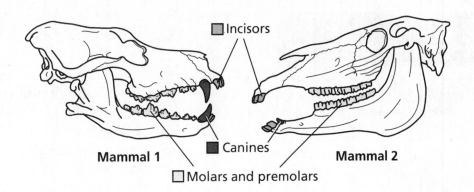

Mammal 1   **Mammal 2**

☐ Incisors
☐ Canines
☐ Molars and premolars

14. The figure shows sketches a researcher made of two mammal skulls. The sketches show the teeth on one side of the jaw. Which phrase describes the most visible difference in the two jaws?

  A The number of teeth

  B The shape of the teeth

  C The names of the teeth

  D The food the animals eat

15. Plants serve as food for some mammals. These animals often have flat teeth that enable them to grind down the tough plant parts. Which animal(s) in the figure above would be able to survive by eating plant materials?

  A Mammal 1

  B Mammal 2

  C Neither animal

  D Both animals

16. You and your lab group are designing an experiment to find the typical pulse rate for students in your grade. Which of the following procedures would be best for you to follow?

  A Also study the pulse rates of students in higher and lower grades to be sure your data are accurate.

  B Study the pulse rates of each student under the same set of conditions, such as after 30 minutes of rest and after 3 minutes of exercise.

  C Have some students rest before their pulse is measured and others do exercise so you'll get a true variety of numbers.

  D Research what the typical pulse rate should be, then find out how many students have that pulse rate.

17. In a process called weathering, water can break down rock. Suppose you want to do a controlled experiment on this topic. Which statement below best describes how you should start?

  A Collect as many different kinds of rock samples as you can.

  B Determine what question you want to investigate, and write a hypothesis based on that question.

  C Determine what conclusion you want to draw, and then figure out how to get your data to match that conclusion.

  D Create a data table and a line graph that will correspond to the data table.

SCREENING TEST, Part 2 *(continued)*

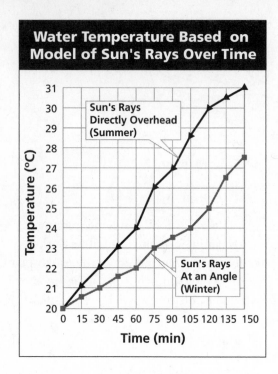

Water Temperature Based on Model of Sun's Rays Over Time

Sun's Rays Directly Overhead (Summer)

Sun's Rays At an Angle (Winter)

Temperature (°C)

Time (min)

18. A scientist set up an experiment to model the position of the sun and its effect on water temperature in winter and summer. The scientist set up 2 containers of water at 20°C, to represent lakes and oceans. She suspended a thermometer just below the surface of the water to measure the temperature. To represent the sun, she placed a light bulb 0.5 m above each container of water. To model winter, one light bulb was placed at an angle. To model summer, the other light bulb was placed directly above the water. Every 15 minutes, the scientist recorded the temperature of each container and plotted the results on the graph above. What kind of information does the graph provide?

A How the temperature of water changes over time

B The effects of time on the temperature of water

C How the presence or absence of sunlight affects the temperature of water

D How increases in water temperature are affected by the angle of the sun

19. Which of the following is the most logical conclusion you can draw from the graph at left?

A Temperatures in the summer are higher than temperatures in the winter because the water temperatures are different.

B When the amount of light is the same, sunlight that shines directly onto water increases the water temperature more than sunlight that shines at an angle.

C Water temperatures in the summer reach about 30°C, while water temperatures in the winter reach only about 27°C.

D Measurements of 120 minutes or more are necessary to determine how the angle of light affects the temperature of water at different seasons.

20. A lab group is investigating this question: "When wind-driven sand particles strike rock, does sand particle size affect how fast rock is broken down?" Which of the following would be the group's manipulated variable?

A Time it takes to break down a given amount of rock

B Mass of sand used

C The size of the sand particles

D The process used to create artificial wind

21. Suppose you are conducting an experiment to determine which metal(s) conduct electric current best. You decide the manipulated variable will be the type of metal wire used. The responding variable will be the current measured in amperes. Which of the following variable(s) should be controlled?

A Length and width of the metal wires

B Cost of the metal wires

C Whether the metal wires react with acid

D How rapidly the metal wires react with oxygen

SCREENING TEST, Part 3, MATH SKILLS

1. Which set of decimals is in order from least to greatest?

   A 5.23, 5.12, 5.1, 5.09

   B 5.23, 5.09, 5.1, 5.12

   C 5.09, 5.1, 5.12, 5.23

   D 5.1, 5.12, 5.23, 5.09

2. Of all of the shirts for sale, $\frac{7}{12}$ have white stripes. Which statement *best* represents this fact?

   A None of the shirts for sale have white stripes.

   B About $\frac{1}{4}$ of the shirts for sale have white stripes.

   C About $\frac{1}{2}$ of the shirts for sale have white stripes.

   D All of the shirts for sale have white stripes.

3. Add.

   $$\frac{3}{9} + \frac{4}{9} = \frac{?}{?}$$

   A $\frac{7}{18}$

   B $\frac{5}{18}$

   C $\frac{7}{9}$

   D $\frac{11}{14}$

4. Benito had $61.65. He earned $31.50 for raking leaves from his neighbor's yard. How much money does Benito have now?

   A $92.15

   B $92.85

   C $93.15

   D $93.85

5. Rosa ran a 100-meter race in 14.74 seconds. Kylie ran the same race in 16.01 seconds. How much faster did Rosa run the race than Kylie?

   A 1.17 seconds

   B 1.27 seconds

   C 2.17 seconds

   D 2.27 seconds

6. Kim has 9 boxes filled with paperback books. Each box holds 68 books. How many books does she have in all?

   A 77 books

   B 448 books

   C 612 books

   D 608 books

7. There are 252 seats in an auditorium. The auditorium is divided into 3 equal sections. How many seats are in each section?

   A 64 seats

   B 74 seats

   C 84 seats

   D 94 seats

8. A gardener planted 8 petunias, 16 lilies, 12 irises, and 24 pansies around the perimeter of a swimming pool. What is the ratio of the number of petunias to the number of pansies in the garden?

   A 1 to 3

   B 4 to 9

   C 5 to 12

   D 3 to 4

SCREENING TEST, Part 3 *(continued)*

9. Which number is a factor of 412?

   A 32

   B 91

   C 103

   D 113

10. James and Paolo both swim 2 kilometers a day. Which measuring tool should be used to determine the swimmer with the fastest time?

   A A scale

   B A clock

   C A meter stick

   D A thermometer

11. The perimeter P of a square may be found using the formula $P = 4s$, where s is the length of each side. The area of a square may be found using the formula $A = s^2$. A square has an area of 64 square meters. What is the perimeter of the square?

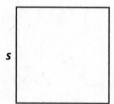

   A 16 meters

   B 32 meters

   C 64 meters

   D 128 meters

12. Use the formula $A = l \times w$ to find the area of the rectangle below.

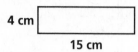

   A 38 square cm

   B 60 square cm

   C 76 square cm

   D 108 square cm

13. A poster lists the average masses of common objects. Which mass would most likely be given in kilograms?

   A A paperclip

   B A dragonfly

   C A young child

   D An orange

SCREENING TEST, Part 3 (continued)

14. What type of data display is shown below?

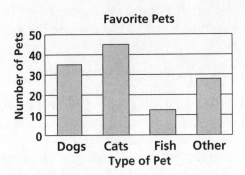

A A table
B A bar graph
C A line graph
D A frequency table

15. On which activity did Carlos spend the most time?

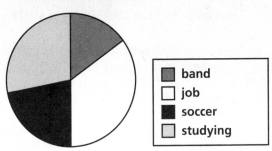

A Job
B Band
C Studying
D Soccer

16. One side of a coin is heads, and the other side is tails. When a coin is tossed 100 times, it will land on tails
A about 50 times.
B about 100 times.
C about 25 times.
D about 75 times.

17. There are 20 marbles in a box: 6 blue marbles, 4 red marbles, 7 yellow marbles, and 3 black marbles. If you reach into the box and choose one marble, which color of marble are you most likely to pick?
A blue
B red
C black
D yellow

18. Solve.

$x + 16 = 52$

A $x = 36$
B $x = 46$
C $x = 68$
D $x = 78$

19. An accountant drives 37 kilometers a day round-trip to and from work. Which expression represents the total number of kilometers she drives after x days?

A $37x$
B $37 \div x$
C $x - 37$
D $x + 37x$

20. Which point represents the ordered pair (1,3)?
A W
B X
C Y
D Z

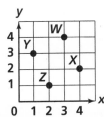

DIAGNOSTIC TEST A, Part 1   LIFE SCIENCE

Directions: *Use the diagram to answer question 1.*

Francesco Redi's Experiment

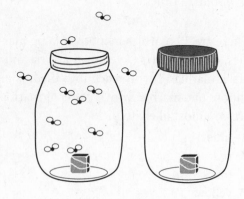

Covered jar is on the right

Meat is in each jar

🪰 = a fly

1. During the mid-1600s, Francesco Redi conducted experiments about the relationship between bacteria and decaying meat. Which statement best describes Redi's conclusion, given the diagram shown?

   A Maggots breed only in decaying meat in a closed jar.

   B Maggots are not spontaneously produced on decayed meat.

   C Maggots breed in most products, but they do not breed in meat.

   D Maggots are spontaneously produced in both covered and uncovered jars.

2. Taylor wanted to conserve water around her home. Which method would save the most water?

   F Watering the lawn at noon instead of watering in the early morning

   G Taking long baths instead of short showers

   H Running many small loads in the dishwasher instead of one large load

   J Keeping water in the refrigerator instead of running faucet water until the water is cold

3. Jeremiah has been studying the experiments performed by Gregor Mendel in his study of inheritance patterns. Jeremiah decides that he would like to test the inheritance patterns of tall and short pea plants. Which statement should be his hypothesis?

   A Pea plants are commonly grown in many gardens.

   B Pollen from the flowers of tall plants is used to fertilize the flowers of short plants.

   C Results of previous studies on pea plants have been inconclusive.

   D If a purebred tall pea plant is crossed with a purebred short pea plant, all offspring will be tall.

GO ON

DIAGNOSTIC TEST A, Part 1 *(continued)*

4. Derrick wants to conduct an investigation to determine which liquid clothes detergent cleans best. What tools will he need to conduct his investigation?

  F Beakers, graduated cylinders, stirring rods, and safety goggles

  G Calculators, petri dishes, and test tubes

  H Computer probes, spring scales, and timing devices

  J Microscopes, thermometers, and balances

Directions: *Use the diagram to answer question 5.*

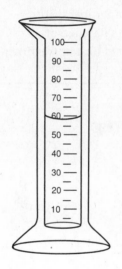

5. What would a graduated cylinder be used to measure?

  A Time

  B Length

  C Mass

  D Volume

6. What measurement is a scientist using a balance probably trying to find?

  F Volume

  G Mass

  H Length

  J Temperature

Directions: *Use the chart to answer question 7.*

	Day Planted	Total Growth by May 10
Green pot	May 1	3 cm
Red pot	May 1	4 cm
Blue pot	May 2	2 cm
Yellow pot	May 4	4 cm

7. Mr. Reid's students planted lima beans during a four-day span. Each plant was given the same amount of water and sunlight. The students measured the growth of the plants each day and collected the data for ten days. Which plant demonstrated the highest daily growth, given the plant's age during the observation period?

  A Green pot

  B Red pot

  C Blue pot

  D Yellow pot

LIFE SCIENCE

GO ON

DIAGNOSTIC TEST A, Part 1 *(continued)*

Directions: *Use the chart to answer question 8.*

Alligator Research: Rate of Eggs Hatched Versus Temperature

Incubation Temperature	Male Eggs Hatched	Female Eggs Hatched
25.2°C	0	95
28.4°C	8	42
30.6°C	51	15
32.8°C	112	0

8. According to the incubation data, what valid conclusion can be made regarding the relationship between temperature and alligator gender?

F More female alligators hatched at warmer incubation temperatures than males.
G Male alligators hatched more often at the coolest incubation temperatures.
H The greatest total number of both male and female alligators hatched at 30.6°C.
J Females hatched best at cool temperatures, and males hatched best at warm temperatures.

Directions: *Use the diagram to answer question 9.*

Pavlov's Experiment on Learning in Dogs

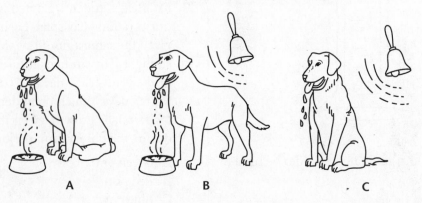

A   B   C

9. After examining the diagram, what conclusion can a student make about Pavlov's experiment?

A The dog will salivate every time the bell rings.
B The dog receives food and salivates, and the bell rings.
C The ringing bell means that the dog will receive food.
D The ringing bell causes the dog to stop salivating.

10. Jill used a Bunsen burner during her laboratory investigation. Which lab rule would be most important during this experiment?

F Move electrical equipment away from the water.
G Wash hands thoroughly with soap and water.
H Never eat or drink anything used in a lab experiment.
J Tie back any loose hair and oversized clothing.

GO ON

LIFE SCIENCE

DIAGNOSTIC TEST A, Part 1 *(continued)*

11. In a field experiment working with plants, which of the following is **NOT** a rule students should follow?

    A Wash your hands thoroughly after handling plants.
    B Use the taste method to identify plant types.
    C Tell your teacher if you are allergic to certain plants.
    D Remove only the leaves and flowers needed.

12. Maria is doing an experiment in which she uses jelly beans to model alleles for a trait. Which lab rule is most important to remember in this situation?

    F Keep chemicals away from the eyes and skin.
    G Wash hands thoroughly with soap and water.
    H Never eat or drink anything used in a lab experiment.
    J Properly dispose of waste as instructed by your teacher.

13. What does the SI prefix *kilo-* mean?

    A 10
    B 1,000
    C 100
    D 10,000

14. If you travel 5 miles, how many kilometers have you gone?

    F 5
    G 10
    H 8
    J 1.6

15. What is the temperature in Kelvin if it is 57°C?

    A 200K
    B 150K
    C 25K
    D 330K

16. Diabetes is a disorder that affects approximately 5 percent of the people in the United States. People with diabetes are not able to produce the correct amount of insulin, which is a protein used by the body. Recent advances in biotechnology have allowed scientists to make bacterial cells that produce usable insulin. Which area of research has given scientists the means to do this?

    F DNA fingerprinting
    G Gene therapy
    H Genetic engineering
    J Selective breeding

17. Many fresh or frozen fruits and vegetables are irradiated with gamma rays before being sold. The radiation slows decay and keeps food fresh for longer periods of time. It also kills organisms that make people ill. In spite of these benefits, some countries prohibit irradiation of food. What possible side effect has led to a concern about food irradiation?

    A Irradiated foods taste better than nonirradiated foods.
    B Irradiated foods promote a healthier immune system.
    C Small amounts of nutrients are lost through irradiation.
    D There is a possible risk of cancer from irradiated foods.

LIFE SCIENCE

GO ON

DIAGNOSTIC TEST A, Part 1 *(continued)*

18. In an attempt to produce electrical energy without burning fossil fuels, large dams have been built on major rivers to support hydroelectric power plants. Although no air pollution is associated with these plants, other negative environmental impacts have been discovered. Which of the following is a likely unintended consequence of damming major rivers?

   F Dams make less water available to surrounding plants upstream.
   G Dams lower the temperature of the water, thereby killing fish.
   H Dams interrupt the paths traveled by salmon as they swim to breeding areas.
   J Dams decrease the area for algae to grow, lowering oxygen levels in the water.

Directions: Use the diagrams to answer questions 19 through 21.

An Animal Cell

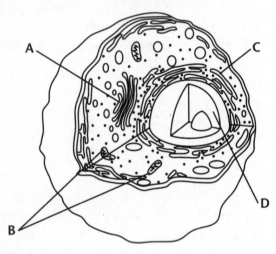

A Plant Cell

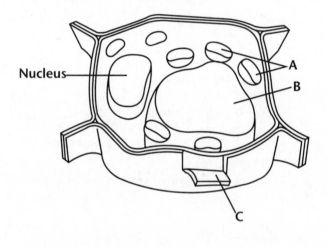

19. Structure B in the animal cell is a ribosome. What is the main function of this structure?

   A To package proteins
   B To provide energy to the cell
   C To transport proteins
   D To direct cell activities

20. Structures A and C in the plant cell are not found in the animal cell. What are the names of these structures?

   F Mitochondria and golgi bodies
   G Chloroplasts and cell wall
   H Vacuoles and cell membrane
   J Nucleus and nuclear membrane

21. In the plant cell, what is the function of Structure B?

   A To store substances
   B To aid in photosynthesis
   C To control cell activities
   D To package proteins

22. What is the function of a cell membrane?

   F To protect and support the cell
   G To perform different functions in each cell
   H To control what enters and leaves the cell
   J To form a hard outer covering for the cell

DIAGNOSTIC TEST A, Part 1 *(continued)*

Directions: *Use the diagram to answer questions 23 and 24.*

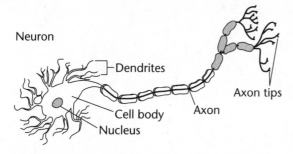

Neuron

Dendrites

Cell body

Axon

Axon tips

Nucleus

23. What is the function of the axon in a nerve cell?

   A Controls all the activities of the neuron
   B Receives messages from the axon tips
   C Sends messages to the dendrites
   D Carries messages away from the cell body

24. What is the function of the dendrites in a nerve cell?

   F Controls all the activities of the neuron
   G Carries impulses toward the cell body
   H Acts as an effector
   J Receives messages from the cell body

25. Which term refers to the movement of water molecules through a selectively permeable membrane?

   A Osmosis
   B Engulfing
   C Diffusion
   D Concentration

Directions: *Use the diagram to answer question 26.*

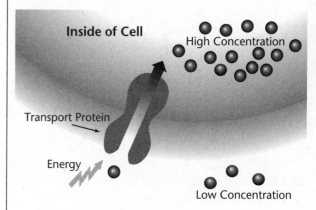

Inside of Cell

High Concentration

Transport Protein

Energy

Low Concentration

Outside of Cell

26. The diagram shows the movement of materials through a cell membrane when energy is required. What is this process called?

   F Osmosis
   G Diffusion
   H Active transport
   J Passive transport

L I F E   S C I E N C E

GO ON

DIAGNOSTIC TEST A, Part 1 *(continued)*

Directions: *Use the diagram to answer questions 27 and 28.*

Cell Division

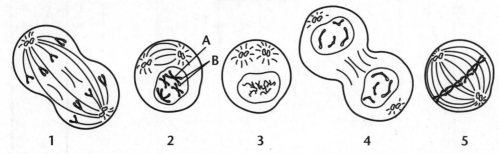

1   2   3   4   5

27. The diagrams show the process by which a cell's nucleus divides to form two identical nuclei. What is this process called?

  A Mitosis
  B Meiosis
  C Interphase
  D Sexual reproduction

28. Which of the following lists the stages of cell division in the correct order, with interphase listed first?

  F 3, 1, 5, 4, 2
  G 1, 2, 4, 3, 5
  H 2, 5, 1, 4, 3
  J 3, 2, 5, 1, 4

29. Jorge wants to know whether music affects plant growth. He puts two identical plants in separate rooms. One room has a stereo that plays rock music all day. The other room is quiet and dark. He waters both plants the same. After two weeks he compares the plants. The plant in the room with music is green and growing. Leaves on the plant in the other room are turning yellow. He concludes that music helps plants grow. What makes his scientific explanation weak?

  A He did not have a testable hypothesis.
  B He did not use two different plants in each room.
  C He did not add fertilizer to the plants in either room.
  D He had more than one variable in his experimental conditions.

30. Binary fission is the bacterial process of

  F producing energy.
  G obtaining food.
  H forming endospores.
  J asexual reproduction.

GO ON

DIAGNOSTIC TEST A, Part 1 *(continued)*

31. What type of reproduction produces fungi that are the same as its parent?

  A Binary fission
  B Budding
  C Fruiting
  D Sexual reproduction

32. A species of bacterium reproduces by binary fission every 15 minutes. Which graph describes the growth rate of a population of these bacteria over a three-hour period?

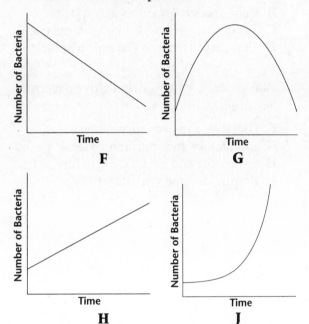

33. What is the process in which a parent cell divides twice to produce sex cells?

  A Cell cycle
  B Mitosis
  C Interphase
  D Meiosis

34. What are chromatids?

  F Identical strands of chromosomes
  G Identical daughter cells
  H Doubled rods of condensed chromatin
  J Pigments that absorb the energy in sunlight

Directions: *Use the graph to answer question 35.*

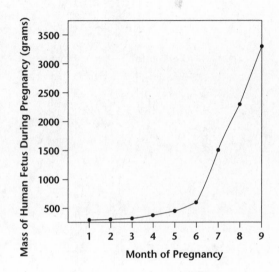

35. The graph shows that the rate at which a developing fetus gains mass

  A remains constant.
  B increases slowly at first and then more quickly.
  C increases at first and then decreases.
  D steadily decreases.

LIFE SCIENCE

GO ON

DIAGNOSTIC TEST A, Part 1 (continued)

Directions: *Use the diagram to answer questions 36 and 37.*

Levels of Organization

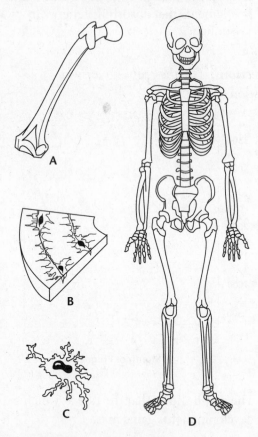

36. What level of organization is represented by Structure D?

F A cell
G An organ
H A tissue
J An organ system

37. Structure B is made up of similar cells working together. What level of organization is Structure B?

A A cell
B A tissue
C An organ
D An organ system

38. Your brain is a structure composed of different kinds of tissue. What is this kind of structure called?

F A cell
G An organ system
H An organ
J A tissue

39. Which of the following lists the levels of cell organization from least to most complex?

A Organs, cells, organ systems, tissues
B Cells, tissues, organs, organ systems
C Tissues, organs, organ systems, cells
D Cells, organs, organ systems, tissues

40. Which organ systems help deliver oxygen to body cells?

F Digestive and excretory systems
G Circulatory and immune systems
H Endocrine and muscular systems
J Respiratory and circulatory systems

DIAGNOSTIC TEST A, Part 1 *(continued)*

Directions: *Use the diagram to answer questions 41 and 42.*

The Respiratory System

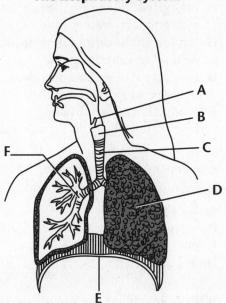

41. What is Structure E?

   A The epiglottis
   B The trachea
   C The diaphragm
   D The larynx

42. Which respiratory system structure closes off the trachea when a person swallows?

   F The epiglottis
   G The trachea
   H The diaphragm
   J The larynx

Directions: *Use the diagram to answer questions 43 and 44.*

The Excretory System

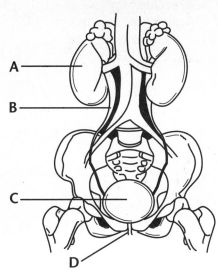

43. What is Structure A?

   A The bladder
   B A kidney
   C The urethra
   D A ureter

44. Structure A is made up of nephrons. What occurs in the nephrons?

   F Urine is formed in the nephrons.
   G Urine is carried away from the kidney in the nephrons.
   H Urine is stored in the nephrons.
   J Blood is deoxygenated in the nephrons.

LIFE SCIENCE

GO ON

DIAGNOSTIC TEST A, Part 1 *(continued)*

45. Perspiration helps maintain body temperature by

A washing bacteria off the skin.
B evaporating and carrying body heat away.
C evaporating and saving body heat.
D preventing heat from entering the body.

Directions: *Use the diagram to answer questions 46 through 48.*

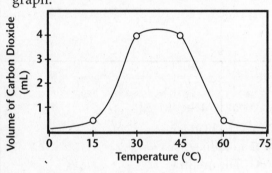

A scientist studying yeast, a single-celled fungus, produced the following graph:

46. Which of these best states the question the scientist was trying to answer?

F How large are yeast cells?
G How does temperature affect yeast activity?
H Do yeast cells grow larger at high temperatures?
J Do yeast cells divide at specific temperatures?

47. At what temperatures do yeast cells produce the most carbon dioxide?

A Between 0° and 15°C
B Between 15° and 30°C
C Between 30° and 45°C
D Between 60° and 75°C

48. How does the production of carbon dioxide by yeast cells change with temperature?

F Production of carbon dioxide decreases with temperature.
G Production of carbon dioxide increases with temperature.
H Production of carbon dioxide decreases as temperature rises and then increases.
J Production of carbon dioxide increases as temperature rises and then decreases.

49. As a person's body loses water, feedback mechanisms cause the person to

A feel thirsty.
B perspire.
C put on a sweater.
D feel tired.

50. What is one thing that adrenaline does to the body during stress?

F It makes the pupils of the eyes become smaller.
G It reduces hearing.
H It stimulates the appetite.
J It increases the heart rate.

STOP

DIAGNOSTIC TEST A, Part 2   **LIFE SCIENCE**

Directions: Use the chart to answer questions 51 and 52.

Type of Immunity	Is It Produced by a Person's Own Body?	How Does a Person Acquire This Type of Immunity?	How Long Does This Type of Immunity Last?
A	?	?	Usually a long time
B	No	Before birth or from an injection that contains antibodies	?

51. What type of immunity is indicated by A in the chart?

  A Passive immunity
  B Active immunity
  C Antibody immunity
  D Allergic immunity

52. How does the body acquire the type of immunity indicated by A in the chart?

  F By coming down with the disease
  G By being vaccinated against the disease
  H Both A and B
  J None of the above

Directions: Use the diagram to answer question 53.

  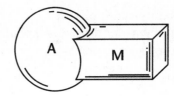

A = antibody   M = measles virus

53. Which of the following describes what is happening in the diagram?

  A Antibodies are destroying pathogens by infecting T cells.
  B Antibodies are destroying pathogens by breaking the cell membranes of pathogens.
  C Antibodies are destroying pathogens by binding to antigens on the pathogens.
  D Antibodies are destroying pathogens by destroying phagocytes.

54. Immunity is the body's ability to

  F distinguish pathogens from one another.
  G destroy pathogens before they can cause disease.
  H fight disease with the inflammation response.
  J produce antigens.

GO ON

DIAGNOSTIC TEST A, Part 2 *(continued)*

LIFE SCIENCE

55. What is the process of heating food or a liquid to a temperature that kills most pathogens?

A Sanitation   **C** Sterilization
B Pasteurization   **D** Inoculation

56. A chemical that kills bacteria or slows their growth is called

F an antibody.   **H** an aspirin.
G an antibiotic.   **J** a decongestant.

57. Medical researchers strive to cure diseases such as AIDS and cancer. Many of them use animals in their testing. Through their tests, researchers learn which drugs work and what dosages are safe. However, a negative consequence to animal testing is that

A animals can be hurt or killed.
B new treatments for diseases are found.
C human lives can be saved.
D animal diseases are cured.

58. The Human Genome Project is a worldwide project to identify the DNA sequence of every human gene. It will provide scientists with a wealth of genetic information about humans. Which technological device will make possible the storage, transfer, and manipulation of this data?

F Computers
G Light microscopes
H Radar sensors
J X-ray machines

59. What is one effect of long-term stress?

A It improves long-term health.
B It makes a person easy to get along with.
C It prevents homeostasis.
D It strengthens immunity.

60. How does exercise help maintain healthy bones?

F By decreasing the need for calcium in the bones
G By decreasing the need for phosphorus in the bones
H By making bones produce stronger outer membranes
J By making bones grow stronger and denser

Directions: *Use the label to answer question 61.*

Nutrition Facts

Serving Size	1 cup (30 g)
Servings Per Container	About 10

Amount Per Serving

Calories 110	Calories from Fat 15

	% Daily Value*
Total Fat 2 g	**3%**
Saturated Fat 0 g	**0%**
Cholesterol 0 mg	**0%**
Sodium 280 mg	**12%**
Total Carbohydrates 22 g	**7%**
Dietary Fiber 3 g	**12%**
Sugars 1 g	
Protein 3 g	

Vitamin A	10%	Vitamin C	20%
Calcium	4%	Iron	45%

* Percent Daily Values are based on a 2,000 Calorie diet. Your daily values may be higher or lower depending on your caloric needs.

61. How much unsaturated fat does each serving of this food contain?

A 0 g   **C** 2 g
B 1 g   **D** 3 g

GO ON

DIAGNOSTIC TEST A, Part 2 *(continued)*

62. According to the Food Guide Pyramid, which group should be eaten in very limited amounts?

F Bread, cereal, rice, and pasta
G Vegetables
H Milk, yogurt, and cheese
J Fats, oils, and sweets

63. An offspring that is the result of asexual reproduction

A has two parents.
B developed from a zygote.
C inherited genes from two parents.
D is genetically identical to its parent.

64. The process by which traits pass from parents to offspring is called

F spontaneous generation.
G cell movement.
H heredity.
J specialization.

65. Genes determine whether you have dimples, what color eyes you have, and even your ability to roll your tongue. What is the role of a gene in inheritance?

A The gene is a section of DNA that controls a trait that the organism inherits.
B The gene contains chromosomes that show an organism's traits.
C The gene has nerves that send messages to the brain controlling specific traits.
D The gene gets messages from its cell about showing certain traits.

Directions: *Use the diagram to answer question 66.*

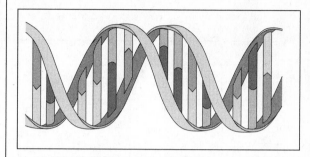

66. Each rung of the DNA ladder is made of

F a single nitrogen base.
G a pair of nitrogen bases.
H a pair of carbon bases.
J a single carbon base.

67. An organism's physical appearance is its

A genotype.
B phenotype.
C codominance.
D heterozygous.

68. An organism's genotype is its

F genetic makeup.
G feather color.
H physical appearance.
J stem height.

69. Scientists call an organism that has two different alleles for a trait

A a hybrid.
B homozygous.
C purebred.
D a factor.

LIFE SCIENCE

GO ON

DIAGNOSTIC TEST A, Part 2 *(continued)*

Directions: Use the diagram to answer questions 70 and 71.

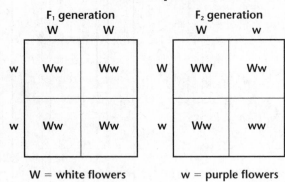

Punnett Squares

W = white flowers   w = purple flowers

70. If flower color is determined by the rules of Mendelian genetics, what is the phenotype of the offspring in the F_1 generation?

F Ww   **H** WW
G Purple   **J** White

71. In the F_2 generation, what percent of the offspring have purple flowers?

A 25%   **C** 75%
B 50%   **D** 100%

Directions: Use the diagram to answer questions 72 through 74.

Pedigree

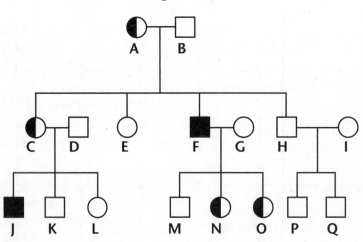

72. In the diagram, circles represent females and squares represent males. Which pairs of individuals in the diagram have children?

F A and B; C and D
G F and G; H and I
H A and B; C and D; F and G; H and I
J P and Q

73. Which individuals express the trait that is traced by the pedigree?

A F and J   **C** N and O
B A and C   **D** A, C, N, and O

74. This pedigree traces a sex-linked trait. Why are sex-linked traits more commonly expressed in males than in females?

F All alleles on the X chromosome are dominant.
G All alleles on the Y chromosome are recessive.
H A recessive allele on the X chromosome will always produce the trait in a male.
J Any allele on the Y chromosome will be codominant with the matching allele on the X chromosome.

GO ON

LIFE SCIENCE

DIAGNOSTIC TEST A, Part 2 *(continued)*

Directions: *Use the chart to answer question 75.*

Blood Types

Blood Type	Combination of Alleles
A	$I^A I^A$ or $I^A i$
B	$I^B I^B$ or $I^B i$
AB	$I^A I^B$
O	ii

75. Blood type is determined by a single gene with three alleles. The chart shows which combinations of alleles result in each blood type. A baby has blood type AB. What can you infer about the baby's parents?

   A Neither has type AB blood.
   B Both have type AB blood.
   C One has type A blood, and the other has type B blood.
   D Neither has type O blood.

76. Genetic disorders are caused by

   F pedigrees.
   G mutations.
   H dominant alleles.
   J sickle-shaped cells.

77. Down syndrome most often occurs when

   A a person inherits a recessive allele.
   B chromosomes fail to separate properly during meiosis.
   C sickle-shaped cells become stuck in blood vessels.
   D blood fails to clot properly.

78. Identical twins Jenna and Joanna are separated at birth. Jenna is raised by a family whose diet includes a variety of foods, including many fresh fruits and vegetables. Joanna's family has a diet that lacks variety; it includes few vegetables and many kinds of junk food. When the twins are reunited 25 years later, what physical difference will likely be present in the twins?

   F Jenna will be taller than Joanna.
   G Jenna will have a darker complexion than Joanna will.
   H Joanna's hair will be straighter than Jenna's.
   J Joanna will have a different eye color than Jenna will.

79. Cloning results in two organisms that are

   A both adult mammals.
   B produced from cuttings.
   C genetically similar.
   D genetically identical.

80. What procedure helps doctors diagnose a genetic disorder before a baby is born?

   F Genetic engineering
   G Selective breeding
   H Amniocentesis
   J Cloning

81. An example of genetic variation in an organism would be

   A fruit without seeds.
   B albinism.
   C presence of dimples.
   D All of the above

GO ON ➡

82. The source of the random variations on which natural selection operates are changes in

   F niches.
   G the Earth.
   H homologous structures.
   J genes.

83. Which is the broadest classification level?

   A Family   **C** Phylum
   B Kingdom   **D** Species

84. One characteristic used to place organisms into kingdoms is

   F how they move.
   G where they live.
   H their ability to make food.
   J their ability to reproduce.

85. Which of the following is **NOT** a characteristic that biologists use to classify animals?

   A The animal's body structure
   B The animal's DNA
   C Where the animal lives
   D The way that the animal develops as an embryo

86. Which kingdom includes only prokaryotes?

   F Moneran   **H** Plant
   G Protist   **J** Fungi

87. Which of the following characteristics do all plants share?

   A Being unicellular
   B Producing flowers
   C Being a prokaryote
   D Being an autotroph

88. Which kingdom includes only multicellular heterotrophs?

   F Protist   **H** Plant
   G Moneran   **J** Animal

89. Which kingdom includes both multicellular and unicellular organisms?

   A Protist   **C** Plant
   B Moneran   **D** Animal

Directions: Use the diagram to answer question 90.

A Bacterium

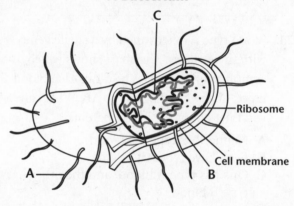

90. Which of the following is found in the cytoplasm of bacterial cells?

   F Cell membrane
   G Nucleus
   H Genetic material
   J Flagella

91. A fungus that is a parasite might feed on

   A a person's skin.
   B a dead tree.
   C bread.
   D wet bathroom tiles.

92. Which phrase describes the size of virus particles?

   F Slightly larger than cells
   G Smaller than cells
   H The same size as cells
   J Much larger than cells

GO ON

DIAGNOSTIC TEST A, Part 2 *(continued)*

LIFE SCIENCE

93. Which of the following is **NOT** a role of bacteria that live in human bodies?

A Digesting food
B Preventing disease-causing bacteria from attaching to the intestines
C Making vitamins
D Preventing diabetes

Directions: Use the diagram to answer questions 94 and 95.

Paramecium   **Euglena**

94. What is the function of the eyespot in Euglena?

F To carry out photosynthesis
G To help the organism identify the direction of a light source
H To produce flagella
J To produce energy for the organism

95. What function does Structure B carryout?

A They help the paramecium move.
B They help the paramecium obtain food.
C They help the paramecium sense the environment.
D All of the above

Directions: Use the diagram to answer questions 96 and 97.

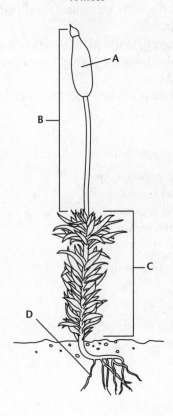

A Moss

96. What does Structure A in the diagram contain?

F Water   **H** Spores
G Food   **J** Leaves

97. What is Structure D in the diagram?

A Rhizoid   **C** Cuticle
B Capsule   **D** Sporophyte

98. Nonvascular plants differ from vascular plants in

F how they make food.
G where they obtain water and nutrients.
H how they transport water and nutrients.
J how they reproduce.

99. Which is **NOT** a characteristic of a plant's vascular tissue?

  A It transports water and food inside the plant.
  B It supports the plant's stems and leaves.
  C It positions the plant's leaves closer to the sun.
  D It transports egg and sperm cells for reproduction.

100. What happens in the phloem?

  F Water moves up.
  G Food moves down.
  H Food moves up.
  J Water moves down.

101. A fern's fronds are

  A leaves.
  B roots.
  C stems.
  D spores.

102. All angiosperms

  F produce cones.
  G produce fruits.
  H are seedless.
  J are tropical.

103. What characteristic do all gymnosperms share?

  A They live only in hot, dry climates.
  B They produce naked seeds.
  C They are trees.
  D They grow cones.

104. The reproductive structures of a gymnosperm are called

  F pollen.
  G ovules.
  H cones.
  J sperm cells.

105. The raw materials of photosynthesis are

  A sugar and water.
  B sugar and oxygen.
  C carbon dioxide and oxygen.
  D carbon dioxide and water.

106. Respiration in most cells requires

  F water.
  G oxygen.
  H chlorophyll.
  J carbon dioxide.

Directions: *Use the diagram to answer question 107.*

107. The flowers in the diagram above are demonstrating

  A a negative plant tropism.
  B phototropism.
  C thigmotropism.
  D a gymnosperm.

108. Germination begins when a seed

  F is dispersed.
  G absorbs water.
  H uses its stored food.
  J grows roots and a stem.

DIAGNOSTIC TEST A, Part 3 *(continued)*

Directions: Use the diagram to answer questions 109 and 110.

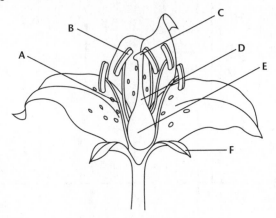

109. A flower is pollinated when

   A pollen falls on the sepals.
   B pollen falls on the stigma.
   C a zygote is formed.
   D pollen falls on the ovary.

110. After pollination, what happens to Structure E?

   F It changes into a fruit.
   G It causes the petals to drop off the flower.
   H It produces more pollen.
   J It causes the sepals to close around the pistils.

111. How do sponges reproduce sexually?

   A Sperm from a sponge fertilize eggs in the same sponge.
   B Water carries sperm from one sponge to eggs in another sponge.
   C Water carries eggs from one sponge to sperm in another sponge.
   D Eggs are fertilized by sperm within the sponge's collar cells.

112. Which of the following is a characteristic of animals with radial symmetry?

   F They have no head or tail.
   G They must move quickly to catch prey.
   H They move faster on land than in water.
   J They have sense organs at the front of their bodies.

Directions: Use the diagram to answer question 113.

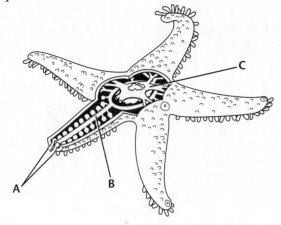

113. How does an echinoderm use Structures A and B?

   A To defend itself from predators
   B To regenerate broken limbs
   C To sense when food is near
   D To capture food and move

LIFE SCIENCE

GO ON

DIAGNOSTIC TEST A, Part 3 *(continued)*

114. Which of the following is a sponge that strains food particles from the water that passes through its body?

    F   **G**   **H**   **J**

Directions: Use the diagram to answer questions 115 and 116.

Characteristics of Arthropods

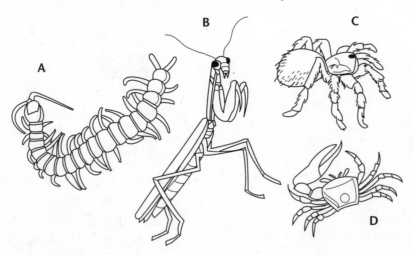

115. Which structure does animal C use to obtain oxygen?

    A Gills
    B Book lungs
    C Moist skin
    D Spiracles

116. Which major group of arthropods is represented by animal A?

    F Insects
    G Centipedes
    H Arachnids
    J Crustaceans

117. At some point in their lives, all chordates have a flexible supporting rod in their backs called a

    A notochord.
    B gill.
    C nerve cord.
    D backbone.

118. Which of the following fish has a skeleton made of hard bone?

    F A shark
    G A ray
    H A goldfish
    J A hagfish

LIFE SCIENCE

DIAGNOSTIC TEST A, Part 3 *(continued)*

119. If an animal is an ectotherm, it has

   A an external skeleton.
   B an internal skeleton.
   C a body that controls its internal temperature.
   D a body that does not produce much internal heat.

120. Most adult amphibians can obtain oxygen through

   F gills and lungs.
   G gills and thin, moist skin.
   H lungs and thin, moist skin.
   J lungs only.

Directions: Use the chart to answer questions 121 and 122.

Characteristics of Birds and Mammals

Animal A	Animal B	Animal C
Cannot fly	Can fly	Can fly
Lays eggs	Lays eggs	Does not lay eggs
Has a diaphragm	Has a gizzard	Has hair
Has webbed feet	Has webbed feet	Has webbed fingers
Has a bill	Has a bill	Has teeth

121. What class of Chordates does animal C belong to?

   A Birds   **C** Mammals
   B Amphibians   **D** Reptiles

122. Which characteristic tells you that animal A is a mammal?

   F It lacks the ability to fly.
   G It lays eggs.
   H It has a bill.
   J It has a diaphragm.

123. What would a grassland located near the equator be called?

   A A prairie   **C** A savanna
   B A taiga   **D** A tundra

124. Which land biome is extremely cold and dry?

   F Desert
   G Tundra
   H Grassland
   J Mountains

125. Which land biome receives less than 25 centimeters of rain per year?

   A A desert
   B A grassland
   C A temperate rain forest
   D A tropical rain forest

126. Oak, maple, and beech trees lose their leaves each year. These organisms typically are found in which biome?

   F Deciduous forest
   G Grassland
   H Boreal forest
   J Tundra

127. In which of the following biomes would you be most likely to find a monkey?

   A Desert   **C** Tundra
   B Rain forest   **D** Grassland

128. Which of the following is a biotic factor in a prairie ecosystem?

   F Water   **H** Soil
   G Sunlight   **J** Grass

GO ON

LIFE SCIENCE

DIAGNOSTIC TEST A, Part 3 *(continued)*

129. Most of Earth's ecosystems ultimately get their energy from

   A the sun.
   B photosynthetic organisms.
   C chemosynthetic organisms.
   D small animals such as insects.

130. The place where an organism lives and that provides the things the organism needs is called its

   F habitat.   **H** community.
   G population.   **J** species.

131. Which of the following is an example of a population?

   A The cats and dogs in your neighborhood
   B The bushes and grasses in a park
   C Rocks in a rock collection
   D The gray wolves in a forest

Directions: *Use the diagram to answer questions 132 through 134.*

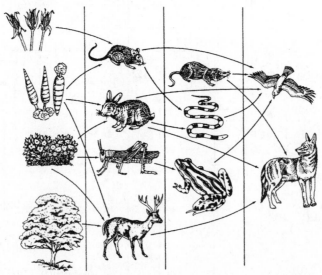

A Food Web in an Area Around a Farmhouse

132. Which producers in this food web are eaten by the largest number of different types of animals?

   F Flowering shrubs and carrots
   G Trees and wheat
   H Flowering shrubs and wheat
   J Flowering shrubs and trees

133. Which animal population would likely decrease if all the grasshoppers were killed?

   A Snakes   **C** Mice
   B Frogs   **D** Coyotes

134. Which food chain would cease to exist if all the flowering shrubs were destroyed?

   F Flowering shrubs ⟶ deer ⟶ coyote
   G Flowering shrubs ⟶ mice ⟶ snake ⟶ hawk
   H Flowering shrubs ⟶ grasshopper ⟶ frog ⟶ hawk
   J None of the above would be affected.

DIAGNOSTIC TEST A, Part 3 *(continued)*

Directions: *Use the diagram to answer questions 135 and 136.*

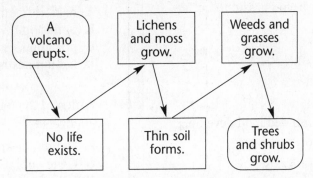

135. Lichens and moss are the first organisms to grow after the eruption. These organisms are known as

   A secondary species.
   B primary species.
   C pioneer species.
   D succession species.

136. This flow chart shows that succession will

   F cause another volcanic eruption.
   G result in a sudden growth of trees.
   H continue to progress after the trees are established.
   J progress in stages that depend on earlier stages.

137. Which is the correct order for secondary forest succession?

   A Weeds and wildflowers ⟶ oak forest ⟶ pine forest ⟶ pine seedlings
   B Pine seedlings ⟶ pine forest ⟶ oak forest ⟶ weeds and wildflowers
   C Weeds and wildflowers ⟶ oak forest ⟶ pine forest ⟶ oak forest
   D Weeds and wildflowers ⟶ pine seedlings ⟶ pine forest ⟶ oak forest

138. The behaviors and physical characteristics of species that allow them to live successfully in their environments are called

   F habitats.
   G limiting factors.
   H biotic factors.
   J adaptations.

139. What did Darwin observe about finches in the Galápagos Islands?

   A Their feathers were adapted to match their environment.
   B Their beaks were adapted to the foods they ate.
   C They had identical phenotypes in all locations.
   D They had identical genotypes in all locations.

140. How does natural selection lead to evolution?

   F Stronger offspring kill weaker members of the species.
   G Helpful traits accumulate among surviving members of the species.
   H Overproduction provides food for stronger members of the species.
   J Environmental changes kill weaker members of the species.

LIFE SCIENCE

GO ON

DIAGNOSTIC TEST A, Part 3 *(continued)*

LIFE SCIENCE

141. If all the members of a species disappear from Earth, the species is said to be

   A extinct.
   B endangered.
   C threatened.
   D limited.

142. A conservation-minded land developer will remember to

   F build plenty of roads.
   G maintain appropriate plant cover.
   H clear as many trees as possible.
   J build houses as far from shopping areas as possible.

143. The loss of a natural habitat is called

   A habitat fragmentation.
   B pollution.
   C poaching.
   D habitat destruction.

144. Which of the following is **NOT** a threat to biodiversity?

   F Habitat destruction
   G Gene pool diversity
   H Pollution
   J Exotic species

DIAGNOSTIC TEST B, Part 1   LIFE SCIENCE

Directions: *Use the diagrams to answer questions 1 through 3.*

An Animal Cell

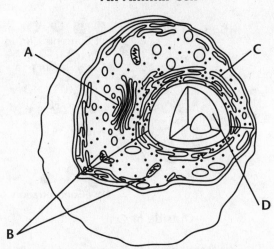

A Plant Cell

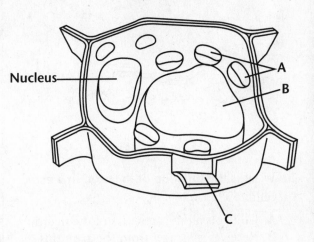

1. Structure B in the animal cell is a ribosome. What is the main function of this structure?

   A To package proteins
   B To provide energy to the cell
   C To transport proteins
   D To direct cell activities

2. Structures A and C in the plant cell are not found in the animal cell. What are the names of these structures?

   F Mitochondria and golgi bodies
   G Chloroplasts and cell wall
   H Vacuoles and cell membrane
   J Nucleus and nuclear membrane

3. In the plant cell, what is the function of Structure B?

   A To store substances
   B To aid in photosynthesis
   C To control cell activities
   D To package proteins

4. Which term refers to the movement of water molecules through a selectively permeable membrane?

   F Osmosis
   G Engulfing
   H Diffusion
   J Concentration

GO ON

DIAGNOSTIC TEST B, Part 1 *(continued)*

Directions: *Use the diagram to answer questions 5 and 6.*

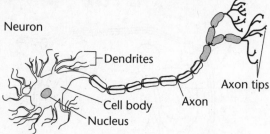

Neuron

Dendrites

Axon tips

Cell body

Axon

Nucleus

5. What is the function of the axon in a nerve cell?

  A Controls all the activities of the neuron
  B Receives messages from the axon tips
  C Sends messages to the dendrites
  D Carries messages away from the cell body

6. What is the function of the dendrites in a nerve cell?

  F Controls all the activities of the neuron
  G Carries impulses toward the cell body
  H Acts as an effector
  J Receives messages from the cell body

7. What is the function of a cell membrane?

  A To protect and support the cell
  B To perform different functions in each cell
  C To control what enters and leaves the cell
  D To form a hard outer covering for the cell

Directions: *Use the diagram to answer question 8.*

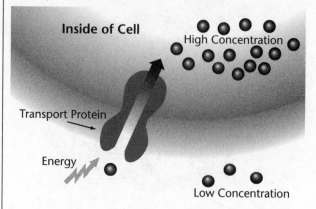

Inside of Cell

High Concentration

Transport Protein

Energy

Low Concentration

Outside of Cell

8. The diagram shows the movement of materials through a cell membrane when energy is required. What is this process called?

  F Osmosis
  G Diffusion
  H Active transport
  J Passive transport

9. Binary fission is the bacterial process of

  A producing energy.
  B obtaining food.
  C forming endospores.
  D asexual reproduction.

GO ON

DIAGNOSTIC TEST B, Part 1 (continued)

10. What type of reproduction produces fungi that are the same as its parent?

F Binary fission
G Budding
H Fruiting
J Sexual reproduction

11. A species of bacterium reproduces by binary fission every 15 minutes. Which graph describes the growth rate of a population of these bacteria over a three-hour period?

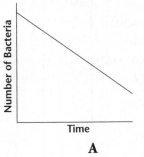

A

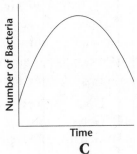

C

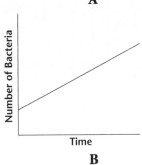

B

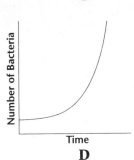

D

12. In a field experiment working with plants, which of the following is **NOT** a rule students should follow?

F Wash your hands thoroughly after handling plants.
G Use the taste method to identify plant types.
H Tell your teacher if you are allergic to certain plants.
J Remove only the leaves and flowers needed.

13. Maria is doing an experiment in which she uses jelly beans to model alleles for a trait. Which lab rule is most important to remember in this situation?

A Keep chemicals away from the eyes and skin.
B Wash hands thoroughly with soap and water.
C Never eat or drink anything used in a lab experiment.
D Properly dispose of waste as instructed by your teacher.

14. Jill used a Bunsen burner during her laboratory investigation. Which lab rule would be most important during this experiment?

F Move electrical equipment away from the water.
G Wash hands thoroughly with soap and water.
H Never eat or drink anything used in a lab experiment.
J Tie back any loose hair and oversized clothing.

GO ON

DIAGNOSTIC TEST B, Part 1 *(continued)*

15. Derrick wants to conduct an investigation to determine which liquid clothes detergent cleans best. What tools will he need to conduct his investigation?

   A Beakers, graduated cylinders, stirring rods, and safety goggles
   B Calculators, petri dishes, and test tubes
   C Computer probes, spring scales, and timing devices
   D Microscopes, thermometers, and balances

Directions: Use the diagram to answer question 16.

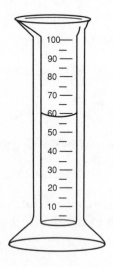

16. What would a graduated cylinder be used to measure?

   F Time
   G Length
   H Mass
   J Volume

17. What measurement is a scientist using a balance probably trying to find?

   A Volume
   B Mass
   C Length
   D Temperature

18. Diabetes is a disorder that affects approximately 5 percent of the people in the United States. People with diabetes are not able to produce the correct amount of insulin, which is a protein used by the body. Recent advances in biotechnology have allowed scientists to make bacterial cells that produce usable insulin. Which area of research has given scientists the means to do this?

   F DNA fingerprinting
   G Gene therapy
   H Genetic engineering
   J Selective breeding

19. Many fresh or frozen fruits and vegetables are irradiated with gamma rays before being sold. The radiation slows decay and keeps food fresh for longer periods of time. It also kills organisms that make people ill. In spite of these benefits, some countries prohibit irradiation of food. What possible side effect has led to a concern about food irradiation?

   A Irradiated foods taste better than nonirradiated foods.
   B Irradiated foods promote a healthier immune system.
   C Small amounts of nutrients are lost through irradiation.
   D There is a possible risk of cancer from irradiated foods.

DIAGNOSTIC TEST B, Part 1 *(continued)*

20. In an attempt to produce electrical energy without burning fossil fuels, large dams have been built on major rivers to support hydroelectric power plants. Although no air pollution is associated with these plants, other negative environmental impacts have been discovered. Which of the following is a likely unintended consequence of damming major rivers?

    F Dams make less water available to surrounding plants upstream.
    G Dams lower the temperature of the water, thereby killing fish.
    H Dams interrupt the paths traveled by salmon as they swim to breeding areas.
    J Dams decrease the area for algae to grow, lowering oxygen levels in the water.

Directions: Use the diagram to answer questions 21 and 22.

Cell Division

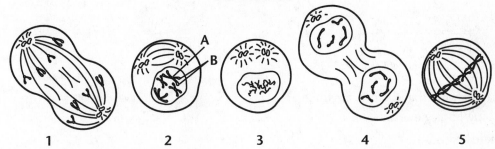

    1   2   3   4   5

21. The diagrams show the process by which a cell's nucleus divides to form two identical nuclei. What is this process called?

    A Mitosis
    B Meiosis
    C Interphase
    D Sexual reproduction

22. Which of the following lists the stages of cell division in the correct order, with interphase listed first?

    F 3, 1, 5, 4, 2
    G 1, 2, 4, 3, 5
    H 2, 5, 1, 4, 3
    J 3, 2, 5, 1, 4

23. Jorge wants to know whether music affects plant growth. He puts two identical plants in separate rooms. One room has a stereo that plays rock music all day. The other room is quiet and dark. He waters both plants the same. After two weeks he compares the plants. The plant in the room with music is green and growing. Leaves on the plant in the other room are turning yellow. He concludes that music helps plants grow. What makes his scientific explanation weak?

    A He did not have a testable hypothesis.
    B He did not use two different plants in each room.
    C He did not add fertilizer to the plants in either room.
    D He had more than one variable in his experimental conditions.

GO ON

DIAGNOSTIC TEST B, Part 1 *(continued)*

Directions: Use the graph to answer question 24.

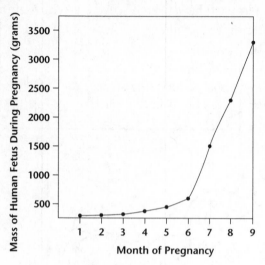

24. The graph shows that the rate at which a developing fetus gains mass

   F remains constant.
   G increases slowly at first and then more quickly.
   H increases at first and then decreases.
   J steadily decreases.

25. What are chromatids?

   A Identical strands of chromosomes
   B Identical daughter cells
   C Doubled rods of condensed chromatin
   D Pigments that absorb the energy in sunlight

26. What is the process in which a parent cell divides twice to produce sex cells?

   F Cell cycle
   G Mitosis
   H Interphase
   J Meiosis

Directions: Use the diagram to answer question 27.

Francesco Redi's Experiment

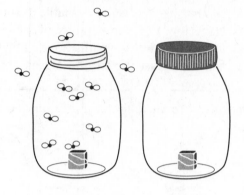

Covered jar is on the right

Meat is in each jar

= a fly

27. During the mid-1600s, Francesco Redi conducted experiments about the relationship between bacteria and decaying meat. Which statement best describes Redi's conclusion, given the diagram shown?

   A Maggots breed only in decaying meat in a closed jar.
   B Maggots are not spontaneously produced on decayed meat.
   C Maggots breed in most products, but they do not breed in meat.
   D Maggots are spontaneously produced in both covered and uncovered jars.

GO ON

DIAGNOSTIC TEST B, Part 1 *(continued)*

28. Taylor wanted to conserve water around her home. Which method would save the most water?

    F Watering the lawn at noon instead of watering in the early morning
    G Taking long baths instead of short showers
    H Running many small loads in the dishwasher instead of one large load
    J Keeping water in the refrigerator instead of running faucet water until the water is cold

29. Jeremiah has been studying the experiments performed by Gregor Mendel in his study of inheritance patterns. Jeremiah decides that he would like to test the inheritance patterns of tall and short pea plants. Which statement should be his hypothesis?

    A Pea plants are commonly grown in many gardens.
    B Pollen from the flowers of tall plants is used to fertilize the flowers of short plants.
    C Results of previous studies on pea plants have been inconclusive.
    D If a purebred tall pea plant is crossed with a purebred short pea plant, all offspring will be tall.

Directions: Use the diagram to answer questions 30 and 31.

Levels of Organization

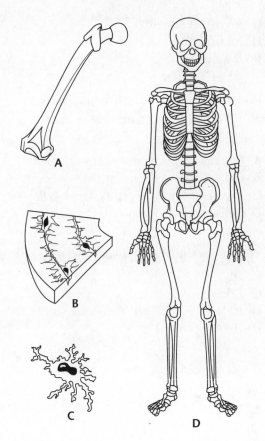

30. What level of organization is represented by Structure D?

    F A cell
    G An organ
    H A tissue
    J An organ system

31. Structure B is made up of similar cells working together. What level of organization is Structure B?

    A A cell
    B A tissue
    C An organ
    D An organ system

LIFE SCIENCE

GO ON

DIAGNOSTIC TEST B, Part 1 *(continued)*

32. Your brain is a structure composed of different kinds of tissue. What is this kind of structure called?

    F A cell
    G An organ system
    H An organ
    J A tissue

33. Which of the following lists the levels of cell organization from least to most complex?

    A Organs, cells, organ systems, tissues
    B Cells, tissues, organs, organ systems
    C Tissues, organs, organ systems, cells
    D Cells, organs, organ systems, tissues

34. What does the SI prefix *kilo-* mean?

    F 10
    G 1,000
    H 100
    J 10,000

35. If you travel 5 miles, how many kilometers have you gone?

    A 5
    B 10
    C 8
    D 1.6

36. What is the temperature in Kelvin if it is 57°C?

    F 200K
    G 150K
    H 25K
    J 330K

37. Perspiration helps maintain body temperature by

    A washing bacteria off the skin.
    B evaporating and carrying body heat away.
    C evaporating and saving body heat.
    D preventing heat from entering the body.

38. As a person's body loses water, feedback mechanisms cause the person to

    F feel thirsty.
    G perspire.
    H put on a sweater.
    J feel tired.

39. What is one thing that adrenaline does to the body during stress?

    A It makes the pupils of the eyes become smaller.
    B It reduces hearing.
    C It stimulates the appetite.
    D It increases the heart rate.

GO ON

DIAGNOSTIC TEST B, Part 1 *(continued)*

Directions: Use the diagram to answer
questions 40 through 42.

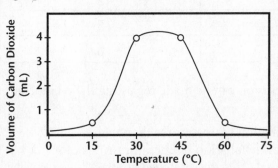

A scientist studying yeast, a single-
celled fungus, produced the following
graph:

40. Which of these best states the question the
scientist was trying to answer?

  F How large are yeast cells?
  G How does temperature affect yeast activity?
  H Do yeast cells grow larger at high
  temperatures?
  J Do yeast cells divide at specific
  temperatures?

41. At what temperatures do yeast cells produce
the most carbon dioxide?

  A Between 0° and 15°C
  B Between 15° and 30°C
  C Between 30° and 45°C
  D Between 60° and 75°C

42. How does the production of carbon dioxide
by yeast cells change with temperature?

  F Production of carbon dioxide decreases
  with temperature.
  G Production of carbon dioxide increases
  with temperature.
  H Production of carbon dioxide decreases
  as temperature rises and then increases.
  J Production of carbon dioxide increases as
  temperature rises and then decreases.

Directions: Use the chart to answer
question 43.

	Day Planted	Total Growth by May 10
Green pot	May 1	3 cm
Red pot	May 1	4 cm
Blue pot	May 2	2 cm
Yellow pot	May 4	4 cm

43. Mr. Reid's students planted lima beans
during a four-day span. Each plant was
given the same amount of water and
sunlight. The students measured the growth
of the plants each day and collected the data
for ten days. Which plant demonstrated the
highest daily growth, given the plant's age
during the observation period?

  A Green pot
  B Red pot
  C Blue pot
  D Yellow pot

LIFE SCIENCE

>GO ON>

DIAGNOSTIC TEST B, Part 1 *(continued)*

Directions: *Use the chart to answer question 44.*

Alligator Research: Rate of Eggs Hatched Versus Temperature

Incubation Temperature	Male Eggs Hatched	Female Eggs Hatched
25.2°C	0	95
28.4°C	8	42
30.6°C	51	15
32.8°C	112	0

44. According to the incubation data, what valid conclusion can be made regarding the relationship between temperature and alligator gender?

   F More female alligators hatched at warmer incubation temperatures than males.
   G Male alligators hatched more often at the coolest incubation temperatures.
   H The greatest total number of both male and female alligators hatched at 30.6°C.
   J Females hatched best at cool temperatures, and males hatched best at warm temperatures.

Directions: *Use the diagram to answer question 45.*

Pavlov's Experiment on Learning in Dogs

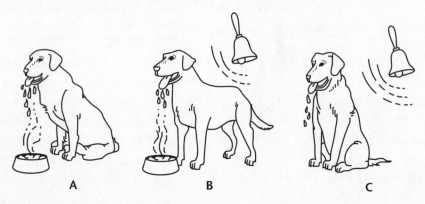

    A   B   C

45. After examining the diagram, what conclusion can a student make about Pavlov's experiment?

   A The dog will salivate every time the bell rings.
   B The dog receives food and salivates, and the bell rings.
   C The ringing bell means that the dog will receive food.
   D The ringing bell causes the dog to stop salivating.

46. Which organ systems help deliver oxygen to body cells?

   F Digestive and excretory systems
   G Circulatory and immune systems
   H Endocrine and muscular systems
   J Respiratory and circulatory systems

GO ON

LIFE SCIENCE

DIAGNOSTIC TEST B, Part 1 *(continued)*

Directions: Use the diagram to answer questions 47 and 48.

The Respiratory System

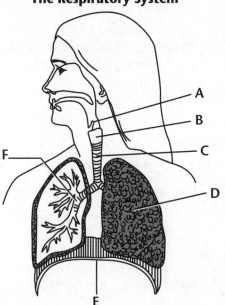

47. What is Structure E?

   A The epiglottis
   B The trachea
   C The diaphragm
   D The larynx

48. Which respiratory system structure closes off the trachea when a person swallows?

   F The epiglottis
   G The trachea
   H The diaphragm
   J The larynx

Directions: Use the diagram to answer questions 49 and 50.

The Excretory System

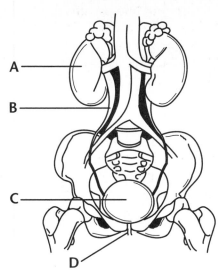

49. What is Structure A?

   A The bladder
   B A kidney
   C The urethra
   D A ureter

50. Structure A is made up of nephrons. What occurs in the nephrons?

   F Urine is formed in the nephrons.
   G Urine is carried away from the kidney in the nephrons.
   H Urine is stored in the nephrons.
   J Blood is deoxygenated in the nephrons.

DIAGNOSTIC TEST B, Part 2   LIFE SCIENCE

51. Which is the broadest classification level?

  A Family   **C** Phylum
  B Kingdom   **D** Species

52. One characteristic used to place organisms into kingdoms is

  F how they move.
  G where they live.
  H their ability to make food.
  J their ability to reproduce.

53. Which of the following is **NOT** a characteristic that biologists use to classify animals?

  A The animal's body structure
  B The animal's DNA
  C Where the animal lives
  D The way that the animal develops as an embryo

54. Which kingdom includes only prokaryotes?

  F Moneran   **H** Plant
  G Protist   **J** Fungi

55. Which of the following characteristics do all plants share?

  A Being unicellular
  B Producing flowers
  C Being a prokaryote
  D Being an autotroph

56. Which kingdom includes only multicellular heterotrophs?

  F Protist   **H** Plant
  G Moneran   **J** Animal

57. Which of the following is **NOT** a role of bacteria that live in human bodies?

  A Digesting food
  B Preventing disease-causing bacteria from attaching to the intestines
  C Making vitamins
  D Preventing diabetes

Directions: Use the diagram to answer questions 58 and 59.

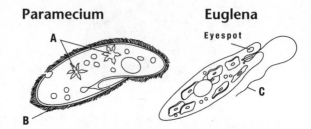

Paramecium   **Euglena**

58. What is the function of the eyespot in Euglena?

  F To carry out photosynthesis
  G To help the organism identify the direction of a light source
  H To produce flagella
  J To produce energy for the organism

59. What function does Structure B carry out?

  A They help the paramecium move.
  B They help the paramecium obtain food.
  C They help the paramecium sense the environment.
  D All of the above

GO ON

DIAGNOSTIC TEST B, Part 2 *(continued)*

60. Which kingdom includes both multicellular and unicellular organisms?

F Protist **G** Plant
H Moneran **J** Animal

Directions: *Use the diagram to answer question 61.*

A Bacterium

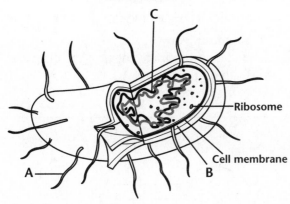

61. Which of the following is found in the cytoplasm of bacterial cells?

A Cell membrane
B Nucleus
C Genetic material
D Flagella

62. A fungus that is a parasite might feed on

F a person's skin.
G a dead tree.
H bread.
J wet bathroom tiles.

63. Which phrase describes the size of virus particles?

A Slightly larger than cells
B Smaller than cells
C The same size as cells
D Much larger than cells

64. Medical researchers strive to cure diseases such as AIDS and cancer. Many of them use animals in their testing. Through their tests, researchers learn which drugs work and what dosages are safe. However, a negative consequence to animal testing is that

F animals can be hurt or killed.
G new treatments for diseases are found.
H human lives can be saved.
J animal diseases are cured.

65. What is the process of heating food or a liquid to a temperature that kills most pathogens?

A Sanitation **C** Sterilization
B Pasteurization **D** Inoculation

66. A chemical that kills bacteria or slows their growth is called

F an antibody. **H** an aspirin.
G an antibiotic. **J** a decongestant.

67. The Human Genome Project is a worldwide project to identify the DNA sequence of every human gene. It will provide scientists with a wealth of genetic information about humans. Which technological device will make possible the storage, transfer, and munipulation of this data?

A Computers
B Light microscopes
C Radar sensors
D X-ray machines

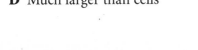

LIFE SCIENCE

DIAGNOSTIC TEST B, Part 2 *(continued)*

Directions: Use the chart to answer questions 68 and 69.

Type of Immunity	Is It Produced by a Person's Own Body?	How Does a Person Acquire This Type of Immunity?	How Long Does This Type of Immunity Last?
A	?	?	Usually a long time
B	No	Before birth or from an injection that contains antibodies	?

68. What type of immunity is indicated by A in the chart?

  F Passive immunity
  G Active immunity
  H Antibody immunity
  J Allergic immunity

69. How does the body acquire the type of immunity indicated by A in the chart?

  A By coming down with the disease
  B By being vaccinated against the disease
  C Both A and B
  D None of the above

Directions: Use the diagram to answer question 70.

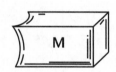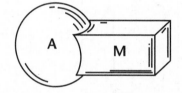

A = antibody   M = measles virus

70. Which of the following describes what is happening in the diagram?

  F Antibodies are destroying pathogens by infecting T cells.
  G Antibodies are destroying pathogens by breaking the cell membranes of pathogens.
  H Antibodies are destroying pathogens by binding to antigens on the pathogens.
  J Antibodies are destroying pathogens by destroying phagocytes.

71. Immunity is the body's ability to

  A distinguish pathogens from one another.
  B destroy pathogens before they can cause disease.
  C fight disease with the inflammation response.
  D produce antigens.

GO ON

DIAGNOSTIC TEST B, Part 2 *(continued)*

Directions: Use the diagram to answer questions 72 and 73.

A Moss

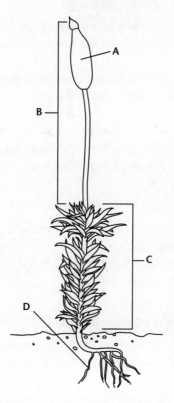

72. What does Structure A in the diagram contain?

   F Water   **H** Spores
   G Food   **J** Leaves

73. What is Structure D in the diagram?

   A Rhizoid   **C** Cuticle
   B Capsule   **D** Sporophyte

74. Nonvascular plants differ from vascular plants in

   F how they make food.
   G where they obtain water and nutrients.
   H how they transport water and nutrients.
   J how they reproduce.

75. Cloning results in two organisms that are

   A both adult mammals.
   B produced from cuttings.
   C genetically similar.
   D genetically identical.

76. What procedure helps doctors diagnose a genetic disorder before a baby is born?

   F Genetic engineering
   G Selective breeding
   H Amniocentesis
   J Cloning

77. An example of genetic variation in an organism would be

   A fruit without seeds.
   B albinism.
   C presence of dimples.
   D All of the above

78. Identical twins Jenna and Joanna are separated at birth. Jenna is raised by a family whose diet includes a variety of foods, including many fresh fruits and vegetables. Joanna's family has a diet that lacks variety; it includes few vegetables and many kinds of junk food. When the twins are reunited 25 years later, what physical difference will likely be present in the twins?

   F Jenna will be taller than Joanna.
   G Jenna will have a darker complexion than Joanna will.
   H Joanna's hair will be straighter than Jenna's.
   J Joanna will have a different eye color than Jenna will.

LIFE SCIENCE

DIAGNOSTIC TEST B, Part 2 *(continued)*

79. The source of the random variations on which natural selection operates are changes in

    A niches.
    B the Earth.
    C homologous structures.
    D genes.

Directions: *Use the diagram to answer question 80.*

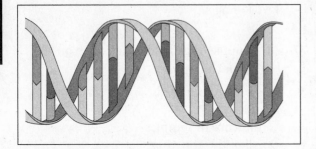

80. Each rung of the DNA ladder is made of

    F a single nitrogen base.
    G a pair of nitrogen bases.
    H a pair of carbon bases.
    J a single carbon base.

81. An offspring that is the result of asexual reproduction

    A has two parents.
    B developed from a zygote.
    C inherited genes from two parents.
    D is genetically identical to its parent.

82. The process by which traits pass from parents to offspring is called

    F spontaneous generation.
    G cell movement.
    H heredity.
    J specialization.

83. Genes determine whether you have dimples, what color eyes you have, and even your ability to roll your tongue. What is the role of a gene in inheritance?

    A The gene is a section of DNA that controls a trait that the organism inherits.
    B The gene contains chromosomes that show an organism's traits.
    C The gene has nerves that send messages to the brain controlling specific traits.
    D The gene gets messages from its cell about showing certain traits.

84. What is one effect of long-term stress?

    F It improves long-term health.
    G It makes a person easy to get along with.
    H It prevents homeostasis.
    J It strengthens immunity.

85. How does exercise help maintain healthy bones?

    A By decreasing the need for calcium in the bones
    B By decreasing the need for phosphorus in the bones
    C By making bones produce stronger outer membranes
    D By making bones grow stronger and denser

86. According to the Food Guide Pyramid, which group should be eaten in very limited amounts?

    F Bread, cereal, rice, and pasta
    G Vegetables
    H Milk, yogurt, and cheese
    J Fats, oils, and sweets

GO ON

DIAGNOSTIC TEST B, Part 2 *(continued)*

Directions: Use the label to answer question 87.

Nutrition Facts

Serving Size	1 cup (30 g)
Servings Per Container	About 10

Amount Per Serving

Calories 110	Calories from Fat 15

	% Daily Value*
Total Fat 2 g	**3%**
Saturated Fat 0 g	**0%**
Cholesterol 0 mg	**0%**
Sodium 280 mg	**12%**
Total Carbohydrates 22 g	**7%**
Dietary Fiber 3 g	**12%**
Sugars 1 g	
Protein 3 g	

Vitamin A	10%	Vitamin C	20%
Calcium	4%	Iron	45%

* Percent Daily Values are based on a 2,000
Calorie diet. Your daily values may be higher or lower
depending on your caloric needs.

87. How much unsaturated fat does each serving of this food contain?

A 0 g   **C** 2 g
B 1 g   **D** 3 g

88. An organism's physical appearance is its

F genotype.
G phenotype.
H codominance.
J heterozygous.

89. An organism's genotype is its

A genetic makeup.
B feather color.
C physical appearance.
D stem height.

90. Scientists call an organism that has two different alleles for a trait

F a hybrid.
G homozygous.
H purebred.
J a factor.

Directions: Use the chart to answer question 91.

Blood Types

Blood Type	Combination of Alleles
A	$I^A I^A$ or $I^A i$
B	$I^B I^B$ or $I^B i$
AB	$I^A I^B$
O	ii

91. Blood type is determined by a single gene with three alleles. The chart shows which combinations of alleles result in each blood type. A baby has blood type AB. What can you infer about the baby's parents?

A Neither has type AB blood.
B Both have type AB blood.
C One has type A blood, and the other has type B blood.
D Neither has type O blood.

92. Genetic disorders are caused by

F pedigrees.
G mutations.
H dominant alleles.
J sickle-shaped cells.

93. Down syndrome most often occurs when

A a person inherits a recessive allele.
B chromosomes fail to separate properly during meiosis.
C sickle-shaped cells become stuck in blood vessels.
D blood fails to clot properly.

LIFE SCIENCE

DIAGNOSTIC TEST B, Part 2 *(continued)*

Directions: *Use the diagram to answer questions 94 and 95.*

Punnett Squares

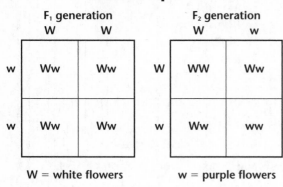

W = white flowers   w = purple flowers

94. If flower color is determined by the rules of Mendelian genetics, what is the phenotype of the offspring in the F_1 generation?

   F Ww   **H** WW

   G Purple   **J** White

95. In the F_2 generation, what percent of the offspring have purple flowers?

   A 25%   **C** 75%

   B 50%   **D** 100%

Directions: *Use the diagram to answer questions 96 through 98.*

Pedigree

96. In the diagram, circles represent females and squares represent males. Which pairs of individuals in the diagram have children?

   F A and B; C and D

   G F and G; H and I

   H A and B; C and D; F and G; H and I

   J P and Q

97. Which individuals express the trait that is traced by the pedigree?

   A F and J   **C** N and O

   B A and C   **D** A, C, N, and O

98. This pedigree traces a sex-linked trait. Why are sex-linked traits more commonly expressed in males than in females?

   F All alleles on the X chromosome are dominant.

   G All alleles on the Y chromosome are recessive.

   H A recessive allele on the X chromosome will always produce the trait in a male.

   J Any allele on the Y chromosome will be codominant with the matching allele on the X chromosome.

DIAGNOSTIC TEST B, Part 3   **LIFE SCIENCE**

Directions: *Use the diagram to answer questions 99 through 101.*

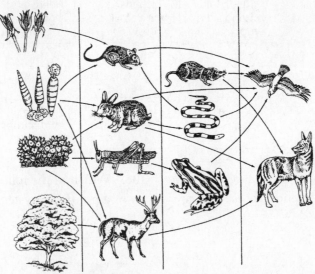

A Food Web in an Area Around a Farmhouse

99. Which producers in this food web are eaten by the largest number of different types of animals?

   A Flowering shrubs and carrots
   B Trees and wheat
   C Flowering shrubs and wheat
   D Flowering shrubs and trees

100. Which animal population would likely decrease if all the grasshoppers were killed?

   F Snakes   **H** Mice
   G Frogs   **J** Coyotes

101. Which food chain would cease to exist if all the flowering shrubs were destroyed?

   A Flowering shrubs ⟶ deer ⟶ coyote
   B Flowering shrubs ⟶ mice ⟶ snake ⟶ hawk
   C Flowering shrubs ⟶ grasshopper ⟶ frog ⟶ hawk
   D None of the above would be affected.

102. Which of the following is an example of a population?

   F The cats and dogs in your neighborhood
   G The bushes and grasses in a park
   H Rocks in a rock collection
   J The gray wolves in a forest

103. Most of Earth's ecosystems ultimately get their energy from

   A the sun.
   B photosynthetic organisms.
   C chemosynthetic organisms.
   D small animals such as insects.

104. The place where an organism lives and that provides the things the organism needs is called its

   F habitat.   **H** community.
   G population.   **J** species.

GO ON

DIAGNOSTIC TEST B, Part 3 (continued)

Directions: *Use the diagram to answer questions 105 and 106.*

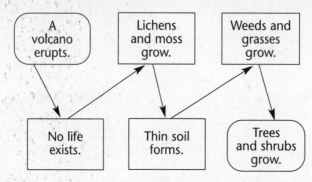

105. Lichens and moss are the first organisms to grow after the eruption. These organisms are known as

A secondary species.
B primary species.
C pioneer species.
D succession species.

106. This flow chart shows that succession will

F cause another volcanic eruption.
G result in a sudden growth of trees.
H continue to progress after the trees are established.
J progress in stages that depend on earlier stages.

107. Which is the correct order for secondary forest succession?

A Weeds and wildflowers ⟶ oak forest ⟶ pine forest ⟶ pine seedlings
B Pine seedlings ⟶ pine forest ⟶ oak forest ⟶ weeds and wildflowers
C Weeds and wildflowers ⟶ oak forest ⟶ pine forest ⟶ oak forest
D Weeds and wildflowers ⟶ pine seedlings ⟶ pine forest ⟶ oak forest

108. Which of the following is a biotic factor in a prairie ecosystem?

F Water   **H** Soil
G Sunlight   **J** Grass

109. At some point in their lives, all chordates have a flexible supporting rod in their backs called a

A notochord.
B gill.
C nerve cord.
D backbone.

110. Which of the following fish has a skeleton made of hard bone?

F A shark
G A ray
H A goldfish
J A hagfish

111. Most adult amphibians can obtain oxygen through

A gills and lungs.
B gills and thin, moist skin.
C lungs and thin, moist skin.
D lungs only.

LIFE SCIENCE

>GO ON>

DIAGNOSTIC TEST B, Part 3 *(continued)*

Directions: *Use the chart to answer questions 112 and 113.*

Characteristics of Birds and Mammals

Animal A	Animal B	Animal C
Cannot fly	Can fly	Can fly
Lays eggs	Lays eggs	Does not lay eggs
Has a diaphragm	Has a gizzard	Has hair
Has webbed feet	Has webbed feet	Has webbed fingers
Has a bill	Has a bill	Has teeth

112. What class of Chordates does animal C belong to?

F Birds   **H** Mammals
G Amphibians   **J** Reptiles

113. Which characteristic tells you that animal A is a mammal?

A It lacks the ability to fly.
B It lays eggs.
C It has a bill.
D It has a diaphragm.

114. If an animal is an ectotherm, it has

F an external skeleton.
G an internal skeleton.
H a body that controls its internal temperature.
J a body that does not produce much internal heat.

115. How does natural selection lead to evolution?

A Stronger offspring kill weaker members of the species.
B Helpful traits accumulate among surviving members of the species.
C Overproduction provides food for stronger members of the species.
D Environmental changes kill weaker members of the species.

116. The behaviors and physical characteristics of species that allow them to live successfully in their environments are called

F habitats.
G limiting factors.
H biotic factors.
J adaptations.

117. What did Darwin observe about finches in the Galápagos Islands?

A Their feathers were adapted to match their environment.
B Their beaks were adapted to the foods they ate.
C They had identical phenotypes in all locations.
D They had identical genotypes in all locations.

118. A conservation-minded land developer will remember to

F build plenty of roads.
G maintain appropriate plant cover.
H clear as many trees as possible.
J build houses as far from shopping areas as possible.

DIAGNOSTIC TEST B, Part 3 *(continued)*

119. If all the members of a species disappear from Earth, the species is said to be

    A extinct.
    B endangered.
    C threatened.
    D limited.

120. The loss of a natural habitat is called

    F habitat fragmentation.
    G pollution.
    H poaching.
    J habitat destruction.

121. Which of the following is **NOT** a threat to biodiversity?

    A Habitat destruction
    B Gene pool diversity
    C Pollution
    D Exotic species

122. Which land biome receives less than 25 centimeters of rain per year?

    F A desert
    G A grassland
    H A temperate rain forest
    J A tropical rain forest

123. Oak, maple, and beech trees lose their leaves each year. These organisms typically are found in which biome?

    A Deciduous forest
    B Grassland
    C Boreal forest
    D Tundra

124. In which of the following biomes would you be most likely to find a monkey?

    F Desert   **H** Tundra
    G Rain forest   **J** Grassland

125. What would a grassland located near the equator be called?

    A A prairie   **C** A savanna
    B A taiga   **D** A tundra

126. Which land biome is extremely cold and dry?

    F Desert
    G Tundra
    H Grassland
    J Mountains

Directions: *Use the diagram to answer questions 127 and 128.*

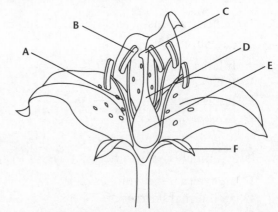

127. A flower is pollinated when

    A pollen falls on the sepals.
    B pollen falls on the stigma.
    C a zygote is formed.
    D pollen falls on the ovary.

128. After pollination, what happens to Structure E?

    F It changes into a fruit.
    G It causes the petals to drop off the flower.
    H It produces more pollen.
    J It causes the sepals to close around the pistils.

LIFE SCIENCE

DIAGNOSTIC TEST B, Part 3 *(continued)*

Directions: *Use the diagram to answer question 129.*

129. The flowers in the diagram above are demonstrating

    A a negative plant tropism.
    B phototropism.
    C thigmotropism.
    D a gymnosperm.

130. Germination begins when a seed

    F is dispersed.
    G absorbs water.
    H uses its stored food.
    J grows roots and a stem.

131. The reproductive structures of a gymnosperm are called

    A pollen.
    B ovules.
    C cones.
    D sperm cells.

132. The raw materials of photosynthesis are

    F sugar and water.
    G sugar and oxygen.
    H carbon dioxide and oxygen.
    J carbon dioxide and water.

133. Respiration in most cells requires

    A water.
    B oxygen.
    C chlorophyll.
    D carbon dioxide.

134. Which is **NOT** a characteristic of a plant's vascular tissue?

    F It transports water and food inside the plant.
    G It supports the plant's stems and leaves.
    H It positions the plant's leaves closer to the sun.
    J It transports egg and sperm cells for reproduction.

135. What happens in the phloem?

    A Water moves up.
    B Food moves down.
    C Food moves up.
    D Water moves down.

136. A fern's fronds are

    F leaves.
    G roots.
    H stems.
    J spores.

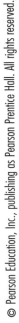

LIFE SCIENCE

Name _____   Date _____   Class _____

DIAGNOSTIC TEST B, Part 3 *(continued)*

137. All angiosperms

    A produce cones.
    B produce fruits.
    C are seedless.
    D are tropical.

138. What characteristic do all gymnosperms share?

    F They live only in hot, dry climates.
    G They produce naked seeds.
    H They are trees.
    J They grow cones.

139. Which of the following is a characteristic of animals with radial symmetry?

    A They have no head or tail.
    B They must move quickly to catch prey.
    C They move faster on land than in water.
    D They have sense organs at the front of their bodies.

140. How do sponges reproduce sexually?

    F Sperm from a sponge fertilize eggs in the same sponge.
    G Water carries sperm from one sponge to eggs in another sponge.
    H Water carries eggs from one sponge to sperm in another sponge.
    J Eggs are fertilized by sperm within the sponge's collar cells.

Directions: Use the diagram to answer question 141.

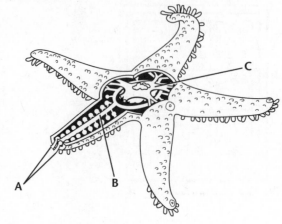

141. How does an echinoderm use Structures A and B?

    A To defend itself from predators
    B To regenerate broken limbs
    C To sense when food is near
    D To capture food and move

GO ON

DIAGNOSTIC TEST B, Part 3 *(continued)*

Directions: *Use the diagram to answer questions 142 and 143.*

Characteristics of Arthropods

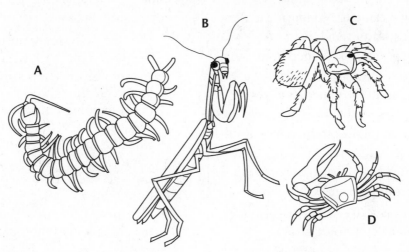

142. Which structure does animal C use to obtain oxygen?

    F Gills
    G Book lungs
    H Moist skin
    J Spiracles

    A Insects
    B Centipedes
    C Arachnids
    D Crustaceans

143. Which major group of arthropods is represented by animal A?

144. Which of the following is a sponge that strains food particles from the water that passes through its body?

    F   **G**   **H**   **J**

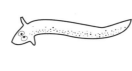

LIFE SCIENCE

DIAGNOSTIC TEST A, Part 1   EARTH SCIENCE

1. The ozone layer protects life on Earth from much of the sun's ultraviolet light. Ultraviolet light can cause sunburn and skin cancer. Scientists discovered that chlorofluorocarbons, gases found in spray cans and air conditioners, appeared to be destroying ozone in the upper atmosphere. Use of these gases was banned because of the hypothesis that banning products with chlorofluorocarbons would replenish the ozone layer. If their hypothesis is true, what result will scientists expect to see?

A Hair spray use will decrease because of the ban on chlorofluorocarbons.

B Ozone will be found at lower levels in the atmosphere, near the ground.

C A decrease in the incidence of skin cancer will result.

D The use of air conditioners will increase.

2. What would be the most appropriate method to find the volume of an irregular shaped object, such as a rock?

F Use a triple-beam balance to compare the mass of the rock with that of other similar objects, and record the data.

G Submerge the rock in a graduated cylinder containing water, and measure the change in the volume of the water.

H Measure the length, width, and height of the rock using a meter stick, and multiply the results.

J Center the rock over the opening of a microscope, and calculate the total magnification of the view.

Directions: *Use the chart to answer question 3.*

Sunflower Growth Chart

Nitrogen Content and Cost	4 weeks	8 weeks	Diameter of Flower Head	Promotion
Brand X: 10% @ $13.79/lb.	3 ft	7 ft	24 inches	$.50 off
Brand Z: 8% @ $13.99/lb.	2 ft	4 ft	18 inches	$1.00 off

3. Sunflowers are different from many other flowers because their seeds take up a large portion of the flower head. When spring arrives, sunflower growers look for ways to enhance their crops and increase their yield. The chart shows the growth rate of sunflowers relative to amounts of nitrogen in fertilizers. Why would Brand X fertilizer be beneficial to someone raising and selling sunflower seeds?

A Brand X has a better sale price than Brand Z.

B Brand X is a well-known brand.

C Brand X produces a 3-foot stalk in 4 weeks.

D Brand X produces larger flower heads.

DIAGNOSTIC TEST A, Part 1 *(continued)*

4. Roland is conducting an investigation of soil texture. Which question should he ask during his inquiry?

   F Does the soil contain nitrogen, sulfur, phosphorus, and potassium?
   G How fast does soil develop?
   H At what rate did the soil form from the bedrock below?
   J Does the soil feel grainy and coarse or smooth and silky?

5. Samantha is examining rock and mineral samples. Which is an observation she might make?

   A Mineral A has a metallic luster.
   B Cubic, orthorhombic, triclinic
   C The rocks containing galena will be heavier than those containing mica.
   D Rock hammer, towel, goggles, hand lens, streak plate

Directions: Use the chart to answer question 6.

Survey Results

87%	Stated no difference in jumping height even though the shoe was very comfortable
7%	Stated the shoe allowed for higher jumps
6%	Unsure of any changes

6. A shoe company is advertising a new athletic shoe with a synthetic rubber sole that they claim allows the wearer to jump 30 percent higher. A test group used the shoe for a three-month period during the regular basketball season. After the three-month trial, the test group was surveyed. From the survey, what can one infer about the synthetic rubber sole of this athletic shoe?

   F The synthetic rubber sole made no significant difference in jumping height.
   G The synthetic rubber sole adds to the design of the shoe.
   H The synthetic rubber sole is durable because it lasted three months.
   J The synthetic rubber sole cost the company too much to continue making that brand.

EARTH SCIENCE

GO ON

DIAGNOSTIC TEST A, Part 1 *(continued)*

Directions: Use the diagram to answer question 7.

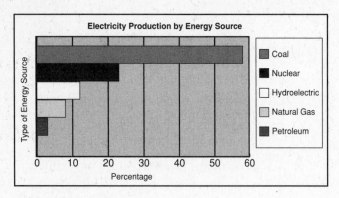

7. According to the data shown, what would happen if coal were no longer available to produce electricity?

A No change in electrical production would occur.

B Petroleum used for electrical production would decrease.

C The primary source of electric power would be eliminated.

D Nuclear power would no longer be used to generate electricity.

Directions: Use the graph to answer question 8.

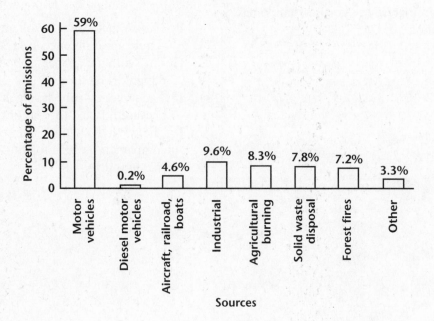

8. Mariah has done some research on carbon monoxide emissions for a class project. Which statement best describes the conclusion that Mariah can make from her research?

F Industrial and solid waste disposal are the main sources of emissions.

G Alternative transportation options should be considered to decrease motor vehicle emissions.

H The number of diesel motor vehicles should be drastically reduced.

J Emmission standards for airplanes, trains, and boats should be strengthend to regulate carbon monoxide emission.

EARTH SCIENCE

DIAGNOSTIC TEST A, Part 1 *(continued)*

Directions: *Use the chart to answer question 9.*

Gases in Dry Air

Gas	Percentage by Volume
Nitrogen	78
Oxygen	21
Argon	0.93
Carbon dioxide	0.036
Neon	0.0018
Helium	0.00052
Methane	0.00015
Krypton	0.00011
Hydrogen	0.00005

9. Elian compiled a chart to represent his research data of gases in dry air. Which graph shows an accurate account of his research?

A
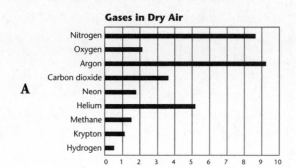

B
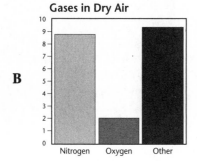

C
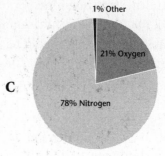

D
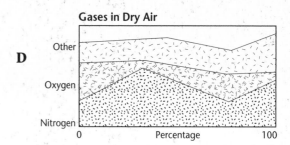

EARTH SCIENCE

GO ON

DIAGNOSTIC TEST A, Part 1 *(continued)*

10. As part of Kay's laboratory investigation, she had to break rocks with a hammer. Which safety rule should she follow?

    F Perform the procedure under a fume hood.
    G Keep chemicals away from the eyes and skin.
    H Protect clothing with an apron.
    J Wear goggles.

11. Brian is experimenting with a stream table. Which safety equipment should he assemble before he begins?

    A Fire extinguisher
    B Paper towels for cleaning up spills
    C Fume hood
    D Bucket for collecting broken glass

12. A group of students is testing rocks for reaction with acid. Bill is in charge of cleaning up after the group finishes. What should he do with the leftover acid?

    F Return the acid to its original container.
    G Check with the teacher for specific disposal instructions.
    H Pour the acid carefully down the sink.
    J Pour the acid into the trash container.

13. What property of an object or substance are the units liter, milliliter, and cubic centimeter used to measure?

    A Weight   **C** Mass
    B Volume   **D** Length

14. How many meters are there in a 10K run?

    F 10   **H** 1000
    G 100   **J** 10,000

Directions: Use the chart to answer question 15.

Prefix	Symbol	Multiple
kilo-	k	1,000
hecto-	h	100
deka-	da	10
deci-	d	0.1
centi-	c	0.01
milli-	m	0.001

15. Which SI prefix means *1,000*?

    A Kilo   **C** Centi
    B Deci   **D** Hecto

16. In an attempt to produce electrical energy without burning fossil fuels, large dams have been built on major rivers to support hydro-electric power plants. Although no air pollution is associated with these plants, other negative environmental impacts have been discovered. Which of the following is a likely unintended consequence of damming major rivers?

    F Dams make less water available to surrounding plants upstream.
    G Dams lower the temperature of the water, thereby killing fish.
    H Dams interrupt the paths traveled by salmon as they swim to breeding areas.
    J Dams decrease the area for algae to grow, lowering oxygen levels in the water.

EARTH SCIENCE

17. The flat, wide area of land along a river is a flood plain. Scientists have studied flood plains and are able to estimate how often floods will occur in these areas. How has this knowledge impacted society?

  A High walls protecting towns have been built along all rivers.

  B Housing developers nationwide no longer build on flood plains.

  C The U.S. government now offers insurance to households in flood plains.

  D Transportation waterways now include flood plains.

18. The Egyptian pyramids (2550 B.C.), the massive stone theater in Greece (500 B.C.), and the 70,000 kg capstone on top of a temple in India (A.D. 1000) all are impressive structures. The fact that those structures were built at all gives evidence of a historical understanding of

  F simple machines.

  G gears.

  H the assembly line.

  J hydraulic power.

Directions: *Use the diagram to answer questions 19 and 20.*

Distribution of Water on Earth

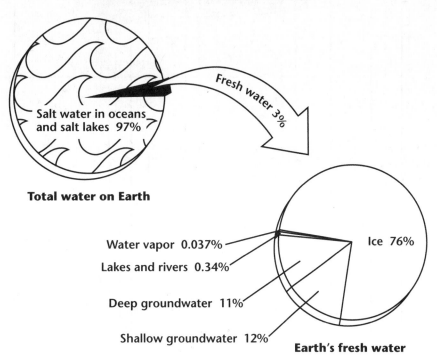

19. What percentage of Earth's total water is fresh water?

  A 97%   **C** 23%

  B 76%   **D** 3%

20. In what form is most of Earth's fresh water found?

  F Water vapor

  G Ice

  H Deep groundwater

  J Lakes and rivers

EARTH SCIENCE

DIAGNOSTIC TEST A, Part 1 *(continued)*

Directions: *Use the diagram to answer questions 21 through 23.*

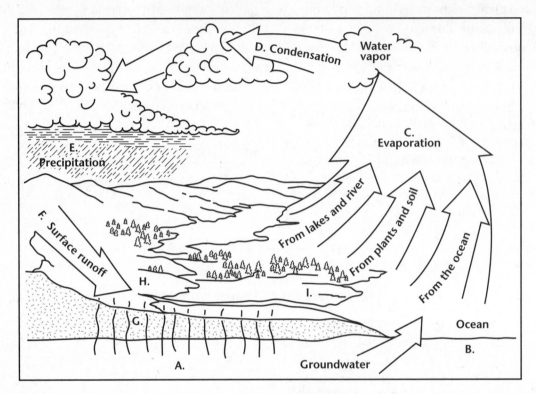

21. Which steps in the diagram involve a change of state?

  A C and D   **C** D and E
  B C and F   **D** A and E

22. Where on Earth's surface does most evaporation occur and most precipitation fall?

  F Plants and soil
  G The oceans
  H The mountains
  J Lakes and streams

23. The energy source that drives the water cycle is

  A heat released by the burning of fossil fuels.
  B the sun.
  C energy from Earth's interior.
  D energy released as water changes state.

24. Salinity is a measure of which of the following in water?

  F Magnesium chloride
  G Oxygen
  H Dissolved salts
  J Sand

25. The most dense ocean water is generally found

  A in the surface zone.
  B in the transition zone.
  C in the deep zone.
  D along the coast.

26. Tides are caused by

  F strong winds that blow over ocean waters.
  G the interaction of Earth, the moon, and the sun.
  H the shifting of the plates on the ocean floor.
  J Earth's revolution around the sun.

DIAGNOSTIC TEST A, Part 1 *(continued)*

27. A large stream of moving water that flows through the oceans is called

   A a current.   **C** a tide.

   B a tsunami.   **D** an undertow.

28. Waves on the surface of the ocean are mostly caused by

   F the moon.   **H** wind.

   G earthquakes.   **J** fish.

29. Which letter identifies the continental shelf?

Directions: *Use the diagram to answer questions 29 through 31.*

Features of the Ocean Floor

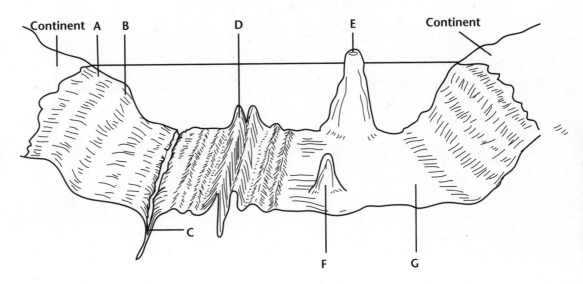

   A A   **C** D

   B B   **D** G

30. The feature labeled D is part of the continuous underwater mountain range that circles Earth. It is called

   F a seamount.

   G the mid-ocean ridge.

   H a trench.

   J an atoll.

31. The feature labeled C represents some of the deepest spots on the ocean floor. These areas are called

   A mid-ocean ridges.

   B abyssal plains.

   C trenches.

   D deep-sea vents.

32. Benthos are organisms that live

   F on the surface of water.

   G throughout the water column.

   H on the ocean floor.

   J in shallow water.

EARTH SCIENCE

GO ON

DIAGNOSTIC TEST A, Part 1 *(continued)*

33. Many organisms that live in the rocky inter-tidal zone are adapted to cling to the rocks to withstand the

    A pounding of the waves.
    B changes in salinity.
    C periods of being underwater and exposed to air.
    D changes in temperature.

34. The only part of the open ocean that receives enough sunlight to support the growth of algae is

    F the intertidal zone.
    G around hydrothermal vents.
    H the deep zone.
    J the surface zone.

35. The ozone layer is part of which of the atmosphere's layers?

    A Troposphere
    B Stratosphere
    C Mesosphere
    D Exosphere

36. Earth's atmosphere traps energy from the sun, which

    F allows water to exist as a liquid.
    G allows solar radiation to penetrate to the surface.
    H allows ozone to form easily.
    J causes meteors to burn up.

Directions: Use the diagram to answer questions 37 and 38.

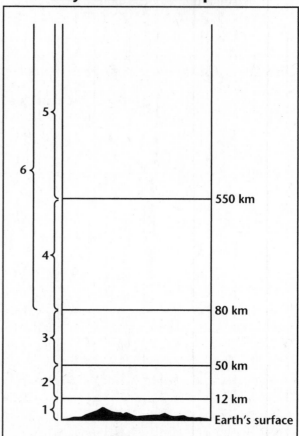

Layers of the Atmosphere

37. From Earth to space, the main layers in our atmosphere are the

    A troposphere, stratosphere, mesosphere, thermosphere.
    B stratosphere, troposphere, mesosphere, thermosphere.
    C mesosphere, troposphere, stratosphere, thermosphere.
    D thermosphere, troposphere, stratosphere, mesosphere.

38. Most weather occurs in

    F layer 1.   **H** layer 3.
    G layer 2.   **J** layer 4.

DIAGNOSTIC TEST A, Part 1 *(continued)*

Directions: Use the chart to answer questions 39 and 40.

Gases in Dry Air

Gas	Percentage by Volume
Nitrogen	78
Oxygen	21
Argon	0.93
Carbon dioxide	0.036
Neon	0.0018
Helium	0.00052
Methane	0.00015
Krypton	0.00011
Hydrogen	0.00005

39. The two most abundant gases in the atmosphere are

 A carbon dioxide and oxygen.
 B carbon dioxide and nitrogen.
 C nitrogen and oxygen.
 D nitrogen and hydrogen.

40. About what percentage of the gases in dry air are made up of substances other than nitrogen and oxygen?

 F About 1 percent
 G About 2 percent
 H About 10 percent
 J About 50 percent

Directions: Use the diagram to answer questions 41 and 42.

North American Air Masses

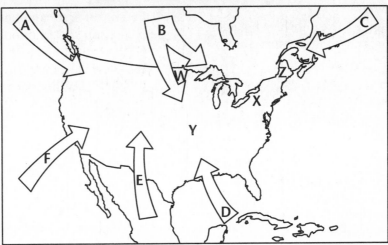

41. Describe the temperature and humidity of air mass A.

 A Cold and dry
 B Warm and moist
 C Cool and moist
 D Warm and dry

42. Which name would be given to air mass E?

 F Continental polar
 G Continental tropical
 H Maritime polar
 J Maritime tropical

EARTH SCIENCE

>GO ON>

DIAGNOSTIC TEST A, Part 1 *(continued)*

Directions: *Use the diagram to answer questions 43 and 44.*

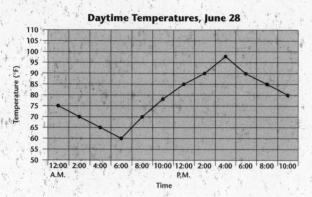

Daytime Temperatures, June 28

43. Study the graph. What is a likely hypothesis for what happened between 6:00 A.M. and 8:00 A.M.?

   A The thermometer was knocked over, changing the temperature reading.
   B Shadows cast on the thermometer caused the temperature to fall.
   C The sun rose.
   D Heat from the stove on which breakfast was cooked caused the temperature to rise.

44. What is a good explanation of why the hottest temperature of the day is around 4:00 P.M.?

   F Exhaust from cars in rush-hour traffic causes the temperature to peak around 4:00 P.M.
   G The moon rises at this time and reflects extra sunlight toward Earth.
   H The sun is at its highest point in the sky at this time.
   J The air started warming as soon as the sun came up and continued warming until it began to set.

Directions: *Use the diagram to answer questions 45 and 46.*

Local Winds

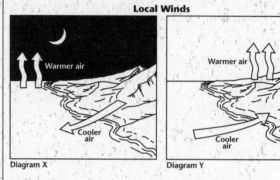

Diagram X   Diagram Y

45. Diagram X shows the formation of

   A a land breeze.
   B a sea breeze.
   C an off-shore breeze.
   D a night wind.

46. What is the main cause of the local winds shown in the diagram?

   F The different amounts of light cast by the sun and the moon
   G Water cooling faster than land
   H Unequal heating of land and water
   J Water heating faster than the land

STOP

Directions: *Use the diagram to answer questions 47 through 49.*

Weather Map

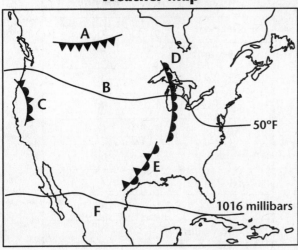

Directions: *Use the diagram to answer questions 51 and 52.*

Temperature Zones

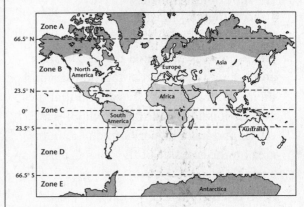

47. What does A represent, and in what direction is it moving?

  A An unmoving stationary front
  B A cold front moving north
  C A warm front moving south
  D A cold front moving south

48. Line B connects points of equal temperature. What is it called?

  F An isotherm
  G A cold front
  H An isobar
  J A warm front

49. As D moves east, temperatures will

  A fall.   **C** stay the same.
  B rise.   **D** all be 50°F.

50. The two main factors that determine the climate of a region are

  F temperature and precipitation.
  G pressure and temperature.
  H altitude and pressure.
  J altitude and temperature.

51. Scientists have divided Earth into several general climate zones. Most of the United States is in Zone B. This is a

  A polar zone.
  B temperate zone.
  C tropical zone.
  D equatorial zone.

52. The climate zones lying between 66.5° and 90° north and south latitude are called the

  F temperate zones.
  G polar zones.
  H tropical zones.
  J subtropical zones.

53. There are many variations within each climate zone. The Great Plains east of the Rocky Mountains has a

  A temperate marine climate.
  B arid climate.
  C semiarid climate.
  D humid continental climate.

GO ON

EARTH SCIENCE

54. The farther you live from the ocean, the more likely your climate will be a
    F   marine climate.
    G   tropical climate.
    H   subtropical climate.
    J   continental climate.

55. Jenna and Jack measured the temperature and humidity at different locations around their school building. They found that the area on the north side of the school is 5°F cooler and has a higher humidity than the area on the east side of the school. This is an example of
    A   a microclimate.
    B   a climate zone.
    C   errors that can occur when reading a thermometer.
    D   poor experimental design.

56. The color of a mineral's powder is called its
    F   streak.   H   density.
    G   luster.   J   hardness.

Directions: Use the chart to answer question 57.

Mohs Hardness Scale

Mineral	Hardness
Talc	1
Gypsum	2
Calcite	3
Fluorite	4
Apatite	5
Feldspar	6
Quartz	7
Topaz	8
Corundum	9
Diamond	10

57. Which minerals in the table will scratch quartz?
    A   Talc, gypsum, and calcite
    B   Fluorite, apatite, and feldspar
    C   Topaz, corundum, and diamond
    D   All of the minerals listed will scratch quartz.

58. Mica breaks apart in flat sheets. This mineral can be described as having _____ in one direction.
    F   fracture
    G   luster
    H   cleavage
    J   hardness

GO ON

DIAGNOSTIC TEST A, Part 2 *(continued)*

Directions: *Use the diagram to answer questions 59 and 60.*

Earth's Interior

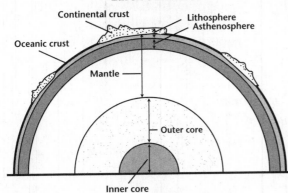

59. What is the correct order (starting from the surface) of Earth's layers?

   A Crust, outer core, inner core, mantle
   B Mantle, outer core, inner core, crust
   C Crust, mantle, outer core, inner core
   D Outer core, inner core, crust, mantle

60. Pressure increases with depth toward Earth's center. In which layer would you expect pressure to be the greatest?

   F Crust   **H** Outer core
   G Mantle   **J** Inner core

61. Which layer of Earth is made up partly of crust and partly of mantle material?

   A Asthenosphere   **C** Lithosphere
   B Crust   **D** Mantle

Directions: *Use the diagram to answer questions 62 and 63.*

The Rock Cycle

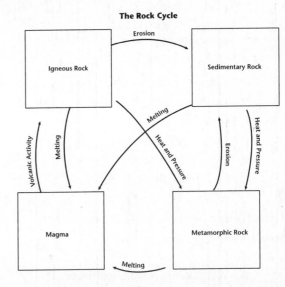

62. Rock that forms from the cooling of magma below the surface or lava at the surface is called

   F sedimentary rock.
   G metamorphic rock.
   H igneous rock.
   J coarse-grained rock.

63. Heat and pressure deep beneath Earth's surface can change any rock into

   A chemical rock.
   B gemstones.
   C metamorphic rock.
   D sedimentary rock.

64. The sedimentary rock formed when water deposits tiny particles of clay in very thin, flat layers is called

   F gypsum.
   G shale.
   H limestone.
   J calcite.

EARTH SCIENCE

GO ON

65. Most rocks formed on Earth's surface are

  A metamorphic rocks.
  B sedimentary rocks.
  C intrusive rocks.
  D igneous rocks.

66. Forces that shape Earth's surface by building up mountains and landmasses are called

  F constructive forces.
  G temperature and pressure.
  H destructive forces.
  J seismic waves.

Directions: *Use the diagram to answer question 67.*

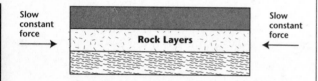

67. The diagram shows forces being applied to rock layers. Which landform will result as the forces are applied?

  A A dip or valley
  B A strike-slip fault
  C A crevasse or canyon
  D A mountain or buckling of rock layers

68. The agent of mechanical weathering in which rock is worn away by the grinding action of other rock particles is called

  F erosion.
  G cracking and peeling.
  H abrasion.
  J ice wedging.

69. The processes that break apart rock and soil and move them from one place to another are called

  A soil erosion and conservation.
  B weathering and erosion.
  C abrasion.
  D erosion and deposition.

Directions: *Use the diagram to answer question 70.*

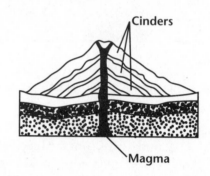

70. The diagram shows the result when ash, cinders, and bombs build up in a steep pile around a volcano's vent. This type of volcano is a

  F cinder cone volcano.
  G shield volcano.
  H composite volcano.
  J dormant volcano.

EARTH SCIENCE

GO ON

DIAGNOSTIC TEST A, Part 2 *(continued)*

Directions: Use the diagram to answer questions 71 and 72.

Soil Development

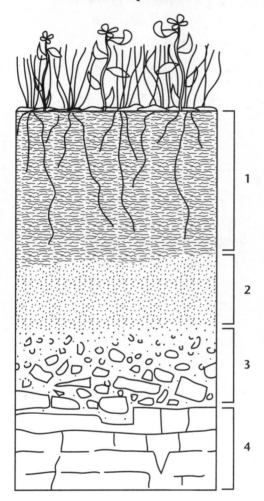

71. The layer of soil in which topsoil is found is

  A layer 1.   **C** layer 3.
  B layer 2.   **D** layer 4.

72. Layer 2 consists of

  F clay, minerals, and little humus.
  G humus only.
  H partly weathered rock.
  J topsoil.

Directions: Use the diagram to answer questions 73 through 75.

River System

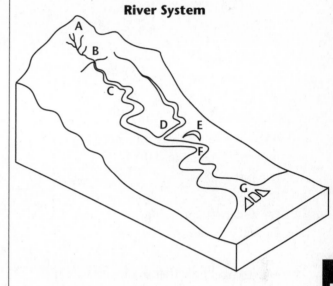

73. Where is the water flowing fastest?

  A A and B   **C** E and F
  B C and D   **D** G

74. The water slows as it reaches letter G. What feature forms just below letter G?

  F A meander
  G A delta
  H An oxbow lake
  J A rejuvenated stream

75. Below letter D, the area surrounding the river is broad and flat. This area is called

  A a coastal plain
  B a delta.
  C a flood plain.
  D an estuary.

76. In the process of sea-floor spreading, where does molten material rise from the mantle and erupt?

  F Along the edges of all the continents
  G Along the mid-ocean ridge
  H In deep-ocean trenches
  J At the north and south poles

EARTH SCIENCE

DIAGNOSTIC TEST A, Part 2 *(continued)*

77. The process by which the ocean floor sinks beneath a deep-ocean trench and back into the mantle is known as

A convection.
B continental drift.
C subduction.
D conduction.

78. The geological theory that states that pieces of Earth's lithosphere are in constant, slow motion is the theory of

F subduction.
G plate tectonics.
H sea-floor spreading.
J deep-ocean trenches.

79. Geologists know that wherever plate movement stores energy in the rock along faults,

A earthquakes are not likely.
B earthquakes are likely.
C an earthquake is occurring.
D an earthquake could never occur.

Directions: Use the diagram to answer questions 80 and 81.

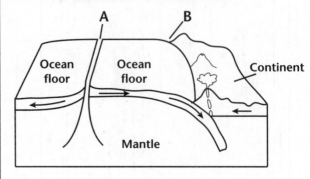

Location of Volcanoes

80. Which type of plate boundary is shown at B?

F Convergent boundary
G Divergent boundary
H Transform fault boundary
J Fractured boundary

81. Earthquakes would most likely occur

A along the boundary marked A, where plates are moving apart.
B along the boundary marked A, where plates are moving together.
C along the boundary marked B, where plates are moving together.
D along the boundary marked B, where plates are sliding past each other.

GO ON

EARTH SCIENCE

DIAGNOSTIC TEST A, Part 2 *(continued)*

Directions: *Use the diagram to answer questions 82 through 84.*

Topographic Map

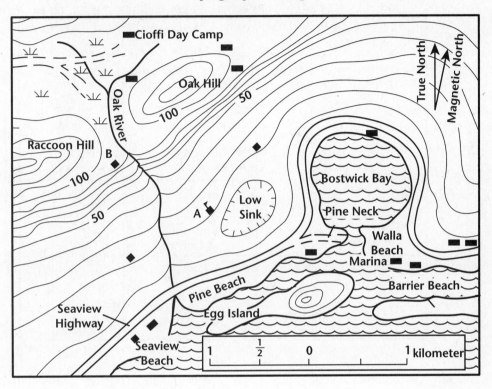

82. If elevation is shown in meters, what is the contour interval of the map?

  F 5 meters   **H** 50 meters
  G 10 meters   **J** 100 meters

83. At high tide during a coming storm, large waves are expected to wash up to the 10 m contour line. Which of the following will be flooded as a result?

  A Cioffi Day Camp
  B Raccoon Hill
  C Oak Hill
  D Walla Beach Marina

84. What is the difference in elevation between the school at point A and the house at point B?

  F 35 meters   **H** 350 meters
  G 70 meters   **J** 700 meters

EARTH SCIENCE

GO ON

Name _____ Date _____ Class _____

DIAGNOSTIC TEST A, Part 2 *(continued)*

Directions: *Use the diagram to answer questions 85 and 86.*

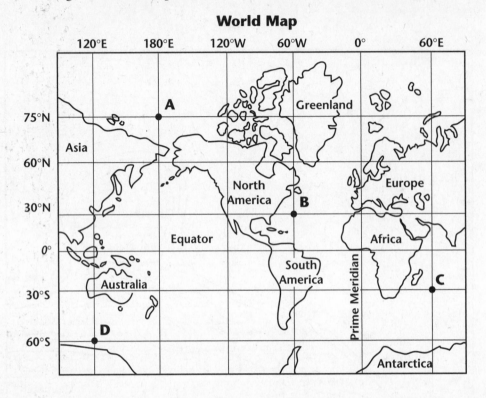

World Map

---

85. A ship is at Point C on the map. What is the exact position of the ship?

   A 30° S, 60° E
   B 30° N, 60° W
   C 60° S, 120° E
   D 75° N, 80° E

86. What is the difference in latitude, in degrees, between points A and D?

   F 75°   **H** 60°
   G 135°   **J** 180°

87. The geologic time scale is a record of

   A the thickness of sedimentary rock layers.
   B the rate of fossil formation.
   C the life forms and geologic events in Earth's history.
   D the time since the extinction of dinosaurs.

88. The law of superposition states that, in horizontal layers of sedimentary rock, each layer is

   F younger than the layer above it and older than the layer below it.
   G neither older nor younger than the other layers.
   H older than the layer above it and younger than the layer below it.
   J always older than any vertical layers.

89. The relative age of a rock is

   A its age compared with the ages of other rocks.
   B less than the age of the fossils the rock contains.
   C the number of years since the rock formed.
   D its age based on how much carbon-14 the rock contains.

EARTH SCIENCE

DIAGNOSTIC TEST A, Part 2 *(continued)*

Directions: *Use the diagram to answer questions 90 and 91.*

Rock Layers

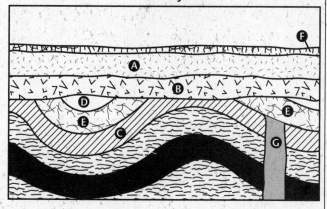

90. What is the age of intrusion G in relation to the sedimentary rock layers through which it passes?

   F Intrusion G is older than the rocks through which it passes.
   G Intrusion G is the same age as the rocks through which it passes.
   H Intrusion G is younger than the rocks through which it passes.
   J Intrusion G may be older or younger than the rocks through which it passes.

91. If rock layers between B and D have eroded away, what is the boundary between B and D called?

   A An intrusion
   B An unconformity
   C A strike-slip fault
   D A reverse fault

92. Radioactive dating enables geologists to determine

   F the age of the atoms in a rock.
   G the half-life of a fossil organism.
   H the relative ages of rocks.
   J the absolute ages of rocks.

Directions: *Use the diagram to answer question 93.*

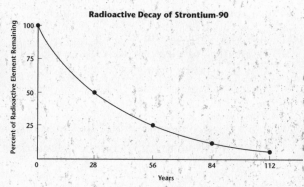

93. Strontium-90 is a radioactive form of the element strontium that undergoes radioactive decay. The graph shows the decay of strontium-90 over time. What is the half-life of strontium-90?

   A 25 years   **C** 50 years
   B 28 years   **D** 56 years

EARTH SCIENCE

94. What is the major source of photochemical smog?

  F Smoke from forest fires
  G CFCs and water vapor
  H Gases from volcanic eruptions
  J Gases emitted by automobiles and trucks

95. Increased amounts of carbon dioxide in Earth's atmosphere may lead to global warming. This, in turn, may lead to

  A more photochemical smog.
  B melting of the polar ice caps.
  C a hole in the ozone layer.
  D less of a greenhouse effect.

96. How can people help reduce the emissions that contribute to smog and the greenhouse effect?

  F By purchasing products that contain CFCs
  G By never pouring chemicals down the drain
  H By taking public transportation or walking instead of driving a car
  J By finding substitutes for garden chemicals

97. Which of the following is **NOT** a major source of freshwater pollution?

  A Human and animal wastes
  B Industrial wastes
  C Wetlands
  D Agricultural chemicals

98. The Waste Recovery Company wants to build a landfill north of Tipp City. Which of these environmental factors should the local county commissioners investigate before they give the company a permit to build?

  F The direction of water drainage
  G The type of soil in the area
  H The depth of the water table
  J All of the above

99. The devices used in cars and trucks to reduce carbon monoxide emissions are called

  A mufflers.
  B catalytic converters.
  C scrubbers.
  D CFC substitutes.

100. Which of the following is a way to reduce water pollution?

  F Installing catalytic converters
  G Finding more CFC substitutes
  H Releasing more heated water from factories and power plants
  J Treating sewage before returning it to the environment

101. What is the most widely used source of renewable energy in the world today?

  A Hydroelectric power
  B Solar power
  C Biomass fuels
  D Tidal power

GO ON

DIAGNOSTIC TEST A, Part 3 *(continued)*

102. Fossil fuels are considered nonrenewable resources because they

   F burn so quickly.
   G are in such high demand.
   H take hundreds of millions of years to form.
   J pollute the air.

103. Solar cells are sometimes used to power all of the following **EXCEPT**

   A calculators.
   B lights.
   C telephones.
   D passenger trains.

104. Which of these is an example of a biomass fuel?

   F Oil   **H** Wood
   G Natural gas   **J** Coal

105. Wind energy is actually an indirect form of

   A electricity.
   B magnetic energy.
   C solar energy.
   D nuclear energy.

106. Energy conservation means

   F slowing down a chemical change.
   G burning a fuel to release energy.
   H using fossil fuels to produce electricity.
   J reducing energy use.

Directions: Use the diagram to answer question 107.

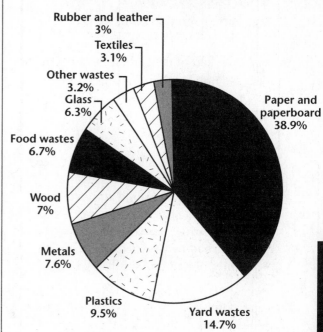

Types of Waste in a Sanitary Landfill

Rubber and leather 3%
Textiles 3.1%
Other wastes 3.2%
Glass 6.3%
Food wastes 6.7%
Wood 7%
Metals 7.6%
Plastics 9.5%
Yard wastes 14.7%
Paper and paperboard 38.9%

107. The Clark County commissioners want to reduce the amount of refuse sent to the local landfill. Which of the following suggestions has the potential to result in the greatest reduction of waste?

   A Recycling glass, plastic, and metals
   B Composting food wastes
   C Reusing rubber, leather, and textiles in new products
   D Recycling paper and paperboard

EARTH SCIENCE

GO ON

DIAGNOSTIC TEST A, Part 3 *(continued)*

108. Day and night are caused by
    - **F** the tilt of Earth's axis.
    - **G** Earth's revolution around the sun.
    - **H** eclipses.
    - **J** Earth's rotation on its axis.

109. Alex worked in the garden for most of the day. He noticed that the length of his shadow changed with the sun's position in the sky. How did Alex's shadow appear around noontime?
    - **A** His shadow was long and stretched toward the western horizon.
    - **B** His shadow was long and stretched toward the eastern horizon.
    - **C** His shadow was very short.
    - **D** His shadow was medium in length and pointed due south.

110. One complete revolution of Earth around the sun takes about
    - **F** one rotation.   **H** one year.
    - **G** one season.   **J** one eclipse.

111. Earth's rotation takes about
    - **A** 365 days.   **C** 24 hours.
    - **B** 6 months.   **D** 1 month.

112. An equinox occurs when
    - **F** neither end of Earth's axis is tilted toward or away from the sun.
    - **G** the north end of Earth's axis is tilted away from the sun.
    - **H** the north end of Earth's axis is tilted toward the sun.
    - **J** Earth's axis is parallel to the sun's rays.

113. Earth has seasons because
    - **A** Earth rotates on its axis.
    - **B** the distance between Earth and the sun changes.
    - **C** Earth's axis is tilted as it moves around the sun.
    - **D** the temperature of the sun changes.

114. In the Southern Hemisphere, the summer solstice occurs when the sun is directly overhead at
    - **F** the equator.
    - **G** 23.5° south latitude.
    - **H** 23.5° north latitude.
    - **J** 30° south latitude.

EARTH SCIENCE

GO ON

DIAGNOSTIC TEST A, Part 3 *(continued)*

Directions: Use the diagram to answer question 115.

The Phases of the Moon

A   B   C   D

E   F   G   H

115. What is the correct order, starting with new moon, of the moon's phases?

  A H, A, E, G, B, F, C, D
  B H, A, B, G, E, F, C, D
  C F, C, D, H, A, E, G, B
  D B, F, C, D, H, A, E, G

116. From new moon phase to full moon phase, you see

  F an increasing amount of the lighted side of the moon.
  G a decreasing amount of the lighted side of the moon.
  H the same amount of the lighted side of the moon.
  J more of the lighted side and then less of the lighted side of the moon.

117. For a solar eclipse to occur,

  A the sun must be directly between Earth and the moon.
  B the moon must be directly between Earth and the sun.
  C the moon must be directly behind Earth.
  D Earth must be directly between the sun and the moon.

118. During what phase can a lunar eclipse occur?

  F New moon   **H** Waxing gibbous
  G First quarter **J** Full moon

119. When are tides highest?

  A During the moon's first quarter phase
  B When the sun, Earth, and the moon are nearly in a line
  C During the moon's third quarter phase
  D When the moon is at a right angle to the sun

120. Tides are caused mainly by

  F Earth's rotation on its axis, which causes water to move.
  G gravitational forces between the land and the water.
  H strong winds blowing water onto coasts.
  J differences in how much the moon and sun pull on different parts of Earth.

121. The two factors that combine to keep the planets in orbit are

  A gravity and orbital speed.
  B orbital speed and mass.
  C mass and inertia.
  D gravity and inertia.

EARTH SCIENCE

⊳GO ON⊳

DIAGNOSTIC TEST A, Part 3 *(continued)*

Directions: *Use the chart to answer questions 122 and 123.*

The Inner Planets

Planet	Diameter (km)	Period of Rotation (Earth days)	Average Distance From the Sun (km)	Period of Revolution (Earth years)
Mercury	4,878	59	58,000,000	0.24
Venus	12,104	243	108,000,000	0.62
Earth	12,756	1	150,000,000	1.0
Mars	6,794	1.03	228,000,000	1.9

122. What generalization can you make from the chart regarding the period of revolution of planets as you move farther from the sun?

   F The closer a planet is to the sun, the longer its period of revolution.
   G The farther a planet is from the sun, the longer its period of revolution.
   H The longer the period of rotation, the longer the period of revolution.
   J Distance from the sun has no effect on the period of revolution.

123. The diameter of Venus is to the diameter of Earth as the period of rotation of Earth is to the period of rotation of

   A Mercury.
   B Venus.
   C Mars.
   D Cannot be determined

124. What do all of the inner planets have in common?

   F They have the same period of revolution.
   G They have the same period of rotation.
   H They have the same diameter.
   J They are small and have rocky surfaces.

125. The asteroid belt is located

   A between Earth and Mars.
   B between Mars and Jupiter.
   C between Jupiter and Saturn.
   D between Saturn and Uranus.

126. Meteoroids usually come from

   F debris from other planets.
   G solar winds.
   H beyond the solar system.
   J comets or asteroids.

127. The most widely accepted theory that astronomers have developed to describe the formation of the universe is called the

   A expanding cloud theory.
   B time warp theory.
   C galactic expansion theory.
   D big-bang theory.

128. Scientists think that our universe is approximately

   F 1 to 5 million years old.
   G 1 to 2 billion years old.
   H 10 to 15 billion years old.
   J 100 to 200 billion years old.

GO ON

DIAGNOSTIC TEST A, Part 3 *(continued)*

129. A light-year is

   A 365 days.

   B the distance light travels in a year.

   C the distance from Earth to Proxima Centauri.

   D the amount of light the sun produces in a year.

130. The distance from Earth to the sun is 150,000,000 kilometers. The distance from Earth to the star Proxima Centauri is approximately 4.2 light-years, or 40,000,000,000,000 kilometers (4.0×10^{13}). Why do scientists use the speed of light to describe distances between stars?

   F Light waves can be detected only from distant sources.

   G Telescopes can detect light-years more easily than kilometers.

   H The speed of light is more easily measured than the speed of sound.

   J Distances between some objects in the universe are too large to use kilometers.

131. How are elliptical galaxies and spiral galaxies different?

   A Elliptical galaxies have almost no gas or dust.

   B Elliptical galaxies vary more in shape than spiral galaxies.

   C Spiral galaxies have almost no gas or dust.

   D Spiral galaxies contain only old stars.

132. The Milky Way Galaxy is a type of

   F spiral galaxy.

   G cloud galaxy.

   H elliptical galaxy.

   J irregular galaxy.

Directions: *Use the diagram to answer questions 133 through 135.*

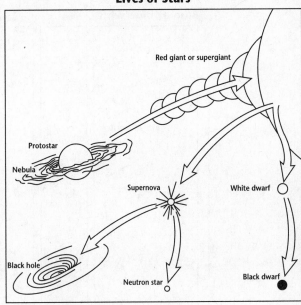

Lives of Stars

133. All stars begin their lives as parts of

   A nebulas.

   B protostars.

   C pulsars.

   D double stars.

134. When stars begin to run out of fuel, they first become

   F red giants or supergiants.

   G supernovas.

   H white dwarfs.

   J neutron stars.

135. The lifetime of a star depends on its

   A temperature.

   B brightness.

   C mass.

   D magnitude.

EARTH SCIENCE

GO ON

DIAGNOSTIC TEST A, Part 3 *(continued)*

Directions: *Use the diagram to answer questions 136 through 138.*

Hertzsprung-Russell Diagram

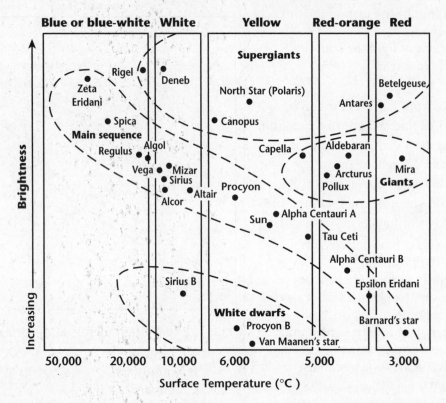

136. The sun is one of a group of stars called

  F the main sequence.

  G supergiants.

  H white dwarfs.

  J giants.

137. Jody used the diagram to compare our sun with Alpha Centauri A. Which statement best describes her conclusion?

  A Alpha Centauri A is slightly cooler and slightly brighter than our sun.

  B Our sun is slightly cooler and slightly brighter than Alpha Centauri A.

  C Alpha Centauri A and our sun are exactly alike.

  D Our sun is hotter and brighter than Alpha Centauri A.

138. Where are the coolest, dimmest stars found on the diagram?

  F In the upper left-hand corner near Zeta Eridani

  G In the center of the diagram near Procyon

  H Anywhere along the main sequence

  J In the lower right-hand corner near Barnard's star

EARTH SCIENCE

GO ON

DIAGNOSTIC TEST A, Part 3 *(continued)*

Directions: *Use the diagram to answer question 139.*

Reflecting Telescope

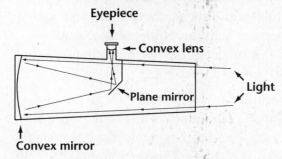

139. A reflecting telescope is designed to

   A break visible light into colors of the spectrum.

   B separate visible light from ultraviolet and radio waves.

   C gather and focus visible light.

   D work better with short-wavelength radiation.

140. Radio telescopes differ from optical telescopes in that they

   F collect and focus visible light.

   G collect and focus radio waves.

   H include an FM radio to which astronomers can listen while they scan the night skies.

   J must be placed in Earth orbit in order to function.

141. The chemical composition and temperature of a star can be determined using

   A a refracting telescope.

   B a spectrograph.

   C a satellite.

   D a reflecting telescope.

EARTH SCIENCE

GO ON

DIAGNOSTIC TEST A, Part 3 *(continued)*

Directions: *Read the passage, and then answer questions 142 through 144.*

Using NASA Technology

You wouldn't wear the outer covering of an airplane to the swimming pool. You wouldn't wear moon boots to a track meet. Indirectly, though, these NASA creations have led to the development of quite a few items of clothing. NASA's Technology Transfer and Technology Spin-off programs encourage private enterprise to use and adapt space research for use in the public and commercial sectors.

The outer covering to an airplane? That technology, developed by NASA Langley Research Center, is riblets. These are small, barely visible grooves that were placed on the surface of an airplane to reduce surface friction and aerodynamic drag. Although the grooves are no deeper than a scratch, they make a surprising difference on the airflow near the plane's surface. Riblets are also featured on a line of competition swimsuits that in testing were found to bring competition results 10 to 15 percent faster than similar swimsuits.

Boots worn on the Moon needed to be specially cushioned because of the unusual lunar surface conditions. The material used has now turned up as a key element in a family of athletic shoes designed for improved shock absorption, energy return, and reduced foot fatigue. Tri-Lock® is the commercial incarnation of a three-dimensional space fabric. The design produces a system that retains shock-absorbing capabilities that stand up to the running, jumping, or pounding inflicted upon the shoe. The Earth-bound athletic shoes reduce impact forces that affect the muscular-skeletal system in the foot and lower leg, just like their Moon counterparts.

---

142. The use of space research in public and commercial applications

    F is illegal.
    G ended after the Apollo program.
    H produces few benefits to society.
    J is called technology transfer.

143. On airplanes, riblets

    A are added to the frame to increase the strength of the airplane in case of a crash.
    B are placed on the wing's surface to reduce friction and aerodynamic drag.
    C are offered as a dinner option on coast-to-coast flights.
    D provide added stability to the wings.

144. An advantage of the three-dimensional fabric being included in some athletic shoes is that

    F it makes the shoes waterproof.
    G it reduces the weight of the shoes.
    H it increases the shock-absorbing power of the shoe.
    J it allows the wearer to jump as high on Earth as the wearer would if on the moon.

DIAGNOSTIC TEST B, Part 1   EARTH SCIENCE

Directions: *Use the diagram to answer questions 1 through 3.*

Features of the Ocean Floor

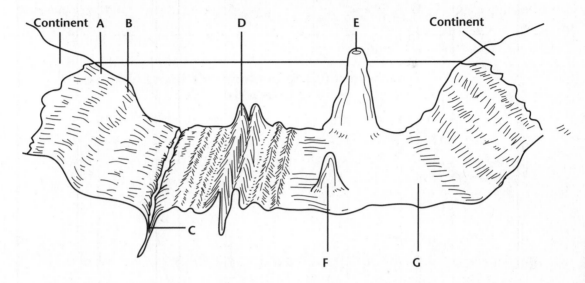

1. Which letter identifies the continental shelf?

   A A   **C** D
   B B   **D** G

2. The feature labeled D is part of the continuous underwater mountain range that circles Earth. It is called

   F a seamount.
   G the mid-ocean ridge.
   H a trench.
   J an atoll.

3. The feature labeled C represents some of the deepest spots on the ocean floor. These areas are called

   A mid-ocean ridges.
   B abyssal plains.
   C trenches.
   D deep-sea vents.

4. The most dense ocean water is generally found

   F in the surface zone.
   G in the transition zone.
   H in the deep zone.
   J along the coast.

5. Tides are caused by

   A strong winds that blow over ocean waters.
   B the interaction of Earth, the moon, and the sun.
   C the shifting of the plates on the ocean floor.
   D Earth's revolution around the sun.

6. Salinity is a measure of which of the following in water?

   F Magnesium chloride
   G Oxygen
   H Dissolved salts
   J Sand

GO ON

DIAGNOSTIC TEST B, Part 1 (continued)

7. Waves on the surface of the ocean are mostly caused by

A the moon.   **C** wind.
B earthquakes.   **D** fish.

8. A large stream of moving water that flows through the oceans is called

F a current.   **H** a tide.
G a tsunami.   **J** an undertow.

Directions: Use the graph to answer question 9.

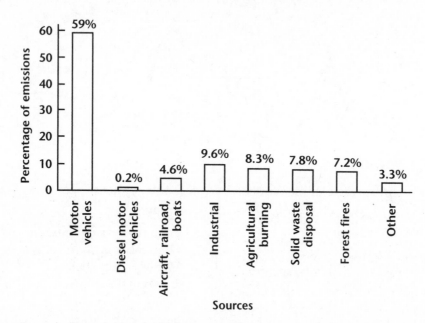

Sources of Carbon Monoxide Emissions in the United States

9. Mariah has done some research on carbon monoxide emissions for a class project. Which statement best describes the conclusion that Mariah can make from her research?

A Industrial and solid waste disposal are the main sources of emissions.
B Alternative transportation options should be considered to decrease motor vehicle emissions.
C The number of diesel motor vehicles should be drastically reduced.
D Emmission standards for airplanes, trains, and boats should be strengthend to regulate carbon monoxide emission.

GO ON

DIAGNOSTIC TEST B, Part 1 (continued)

Directions: *Use the chart to answer question 10.*

Gases in Dry Air

Gas	Percentage by Volume
Nitrogen	78
Oxygen	21
Argon	0.93
Carbon dioxide	0.036
Neon	0.0018
Helium	0.00052
Methane	0.00015
Krypton	0.00011
Hydrogen	0.00005

10. Elian compiled a chart to represent his research data of gases in dry air.
Which graph shows an accurate account of his research?

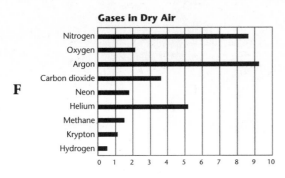

F

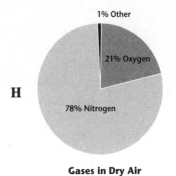

H

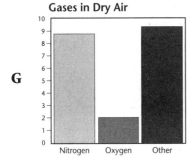

G

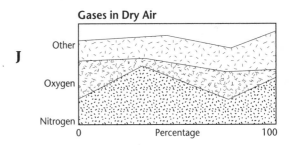

J

EARTH SCIENCE

>GO ON>

DIAGNOSTIC TEST B, Part 1 *(continued)*

Directions: Use the diagram to answer question 11.

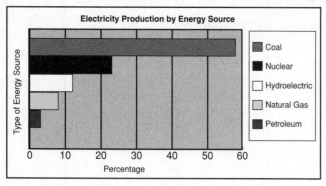

11. According to the data shown, what would happen if coal were no longer available to produce electricity?

A No change in electrical production would occur.

B Petroleum used for electrical production would decrease.

C The primary source of electric power would be eliminated.

D Nuclear power would no longer be used to generate electricity.

Directions: Use the diagram to answer questions 12 and 13.

Distribution of Water on Earth

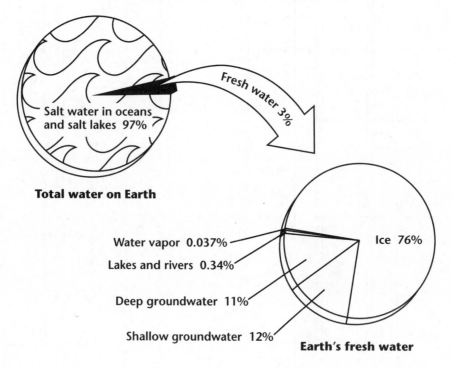

12. What percentage of Earth's total water is fresh water?

F 97% **H** 23%

G 76% **J** 3%

13. In what form is most of Earth's fresh water found?

A Water vapor

B Ice

C Deep groundwater

D Lakes and rivers

> GO ON

DIAGNOSTIC TEST B, Part 1 *(continued)*

Directions: *Use the diagram to answer questions 14 through 16.*

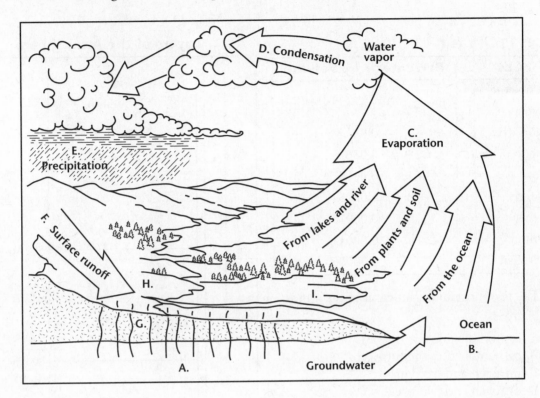

14. Which steps in the diagram involve a change of state?

   F C and D   **H** D and E
   G C and F   **J** A and E

15. Where on Earth's surface does most evaporation occur and most precipitation fall?

   A Plants and soil
   B The oceans
   C The mountains
   D Lakes and streams

16. The energy source that drives the water cycle is

   F heat released by the burning of fossil fuels.
   G the sun.
   H energy from Earth's interior.
   J energy released as water changes state.

17. The ozone layer is part of which of the atmosphere's layers?

   A Troposphere
   B Stratosphere
   C Mesosphere
   D Exosphere

18. Earth's atmosphere traps energy from the sun, which

   F allows water to exist as a liquid.
   G allows solar radiation to penetrate to the surface.
   H allows ozone to form easily.
   J causes meteors to burn up.

EARTH SCIENCE

GO ON

DIAGNOSTIC TEST B, Part 1 (continued)

Directions: *Use the chart to answer questions 19 and 20.*

Gases in Dry Air

Gas	Percentage by Volume
Nitrogen	78
Oxygen	21
Argon	0.93
Carbon dioxide	0.036
Neon	0.0018
Helium	0.00052
Methane	0.00015
Krypton	0.00011
Hydrogen	0.00005

19. The two most abundant gases in the atmosphere are

  A carbon dioxide and oxygen.
  B carbon dioxide and nitrogen.
  C nitrogen and oxygen.
  D nitrogen and hydrogen.

20. About what percentage of the gases in dry air are made up of substances other than nitrogen and oxygen?

  F About 1 percent
  G About 2 percent
  H About 10 percent
  J About 50 percent

Directions: *Use the diagram to answer questions 21 and 22.*

Layers of the Atmosphere

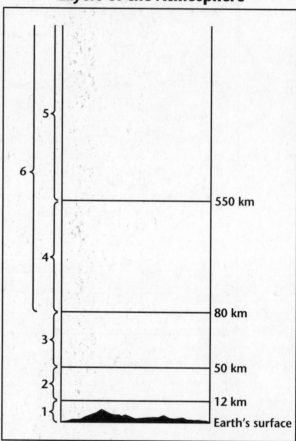

21. From Earth to space, the main layers in our atmosphere are the

  A troposphere, stratosphere, mesosphere, thermosphere.
  B stratosphere, troposphere, mesosphere, thermosphere.
  C mesosphere, troposphere, stratosphere, thermosphere.
  D thermosphere, troposphere, stratosphere, mesosphere.

22. Most weather occurs in

  F layer 1.   **H** layer 3.
  G layer 2.   **J** layer 4.

EARTH SCIENCE

DIAGNOSTIC TEST B, Part 1 *(continued)*

Directions: Use the chart to answer question 23.

Survey Results

87%	Stated no difference in jumping height even though the shoe was very comfortable
7%	Stated the shoe allowed for higher jumps
6%	Unsure of any changes

23. A shoe company is advertising a new athletic shoe with a synthetic rubber sole that they claim allows the wearer to jump 30 percent higher. A test group used the shoe for a three-month period during the regular basketball season. After the three-month trial, the test group was surveyed. From the survey, what can one infer about the synthetic rubber sole of this athletic shoe?

   A The synthetic rubber sole made no significant difference in jumping height.

   B The synthetic rubber sole adds to the design of the shoe.

   C The synthetic rubber sole is durable because it lasted three months.

   D The synthetic rubber sole cost the company too much to continue making that brand.

24. Roland is conducting an investigation of soil texture. Which question should he ask during his inquiry?

   F Does the soil contain nitrogen, sulfur, phosphorus, and potassium?

   G How fast does soil develop?

   H At what rate did the soil form from the bedrock below?

   J Does the soil feel grainy and coarse or smooth and silky?

25. Samantha is examining rock and mineral samples. Which is an observation she might make?

   A Mineral A has a metallic luster.

   B Cubic, orthorhombic, triclinic

   C The rocks containing galena will be heavier than those containing mica.

   D Rock hammer, towel, goggles, hand lens, streak plate

26. The Egyptian pyramids (2550 B.C.), the massive stone theater in Greece (500 B.C.), and the 70,000 kg capstone on top of a temple in India (A.D. 1000) all are impressive structures. The fact that those structures were built at all gives evidence of a historical understanding of

   F simple machines.

   G gears.

   H the assembly line.

   J hydraulic power.

27. The flat, wide area of land along a river is a flood plain. Scientists have studied flood plains and are able to estimate how often floods will occur in these areas. How has this knowledge impacted society?

   A High walls protecting towns have been built along all rivers.

   B Housing developers nationwide no longer build on flood plains.

   C The U.S. government now offers insurance to households in flood plains.

   D Transportation waterways now include flood plains.

EARTH SCIENCE

GO ON

28. In an attempt to produce electrical energy without burning fossil fuels, large dams have been built on major rivers to support hydroelectric power plants. Although no air pollution is associated with these plants, other negative environmental impacts have been discovered. Which of the following is a likely unintended consequence of damming major rivers?

F Dams make less water available to surrounding plants upstream.

G Dams lower the temperature of the water, thereby killing fish.

H Dams interrupt the paths traveled by salmon as they swim to breeding areas.

J Dams decrease the area for algae to grow, lowering oxygen levels in the water.

29. The ozone layer protects life on Earth from much of the sun's ultraviolet light. Ultraviolet light can cause sunburn and skin cancer. Scientists discovered that chlorofluorocarbons, gases found in spray cans and air conditioners, appeared to be destroying ozone in the upper atmosphere. Use of these gases was banned because of the hypothesis that banning products with chlorofluorocarbons would replenish the ozone layer. If their hypothesis is true, what result will scientists expect to see?

A Hair spray use will decrease because of the ban on chlorofluorocarbons.

B Ozone will be found at lower levels in the atmosphere, near the ground.

C A decrease in the incidence of skin cancer will result.

D The use of air conditioners will increase.

Directions: Use the chart to answer question 30.

Sunflower Growth Chart

Nitrogen Content and Cost	4 weeks	8 weeks	Diameter of Flower Head	Promotion
Brand X: 10% @ $13.79/lb.	3 ft	7 ft	24 inches	$.50 off
Brand Z: 8% @ $13.99/lb.	2 ft	4 ft	18 inches	$1.00 off

30. Sunflowers are different from many other flowers because their seeds take up a large portion of the flower head. When spring arrives, sunflower growers look for ways to enhance their crops and increase their yield. The chart shows the growth rate of sunflowers relative to amounts of nitrogen in fertilizers. Why would Brand X fertilizer be beneficial to someone raising and selling sunflower seeds?

F Brand X has a better sale price than Brand Z.

G Brand X is a well-known brand.

H Brand X produces a 3-foot stalk in 4 weeks.

J Brand X produces larger flower heads.

GO ON

DIAGNOSTIC TEST B, Part 1 *(continued)*

31. What would be the most appropriate method to find the volume of an irregular shaped object, such as a rock?

   A Use a triple-beam balance to compare the mass of the rock with that of other similar objects, and record the data.

   B Submerge the rock in a graduated cylinder containing water, and measure the change in the volume of the water.

   C Measure the length, width, and height of the rock using a meter stick, and multiply the results.

   D Center the rock over the opening of a microscope, and calculate the total magnification of the view.

Directions: Use the chart to answer question 32.

Prefix	Symbol	Multiple
kilo-	k	1,000
hecto-	h	100
deka-	da	10
deci-	d	0.1
centi-	c	0.01
milli-	m	0.001

32. Which SI prefix means *1,000*?

   F Kilo   **H** Centi

   G Deci   **J** Hecto

33. How many meters are there in a 10K run?

   A 10   **C** 1000

   B 100   **D** 10,000

34. What property of an object or substance are the units liter, milliliter, and cubic centimeter used to measure?

   F Weight   **H** Mass

   G Volume   **J** Length

35. Many organisms that live in the rocky intertidal zone are adapted to cling to the rocks to withstand the

   A pounding of the waves.

   B changes in salinity.

   C periods of being underwater and exposed to air.

   D changes in temperature.

36. The only part of the open ocean that receives enough sunlight to support the growth of algae is

   F the intertidal zone.

   G around hydrothermal vents.

   H the deep zone.

   J the surface zone.

37. Benthos are organisms that live

   A on the surface of water.

   B throughout the water column.

   C on the ocean floor.

   D in shallow water.

EARTH SCIENCE

GO ON

DIAGNOSTIC TEST B, Part 1 *(continued)*

38. As part of Kay's laboratory investigation, she had to break rocks with a hammer. Which safety rule should she follow?

   F Perform the procedure under a fume hood.

   G Keep chemicals away from the eyes and skin.

   H Protect clothing with an apron.

   J Wear goggles.

39. Brian is experimenting with a stream table. Which safety equipment should he assemble before he begins?

   A Fire extinguisher

   B Paper towels for cleaning up spills

   C Fume hood

   D Bucket for collecting broken glass

40. A group of students is testing rocks for reaction with acid. Bill is in charge of cleaning up after the group finishes. What should he do with the leftover acid?

   F Return the acid to its original container.

   G Check with the teacher for specific disposal instructions.

   H Pour the acid carefully down the sink.

   J Pour the acid into the trash container.

Directions: Use the diagram to answer questions 41 and 42.

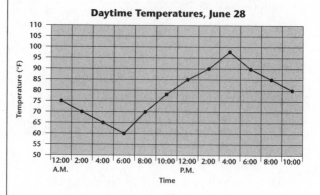

41. Study the graph. What is a likely hypothesis for what happened between 6:00 A.M. and 8:00 A.M.?

   A The thermometer was knocked over, changing the temperature reading.

   B Shadows cast on the thermometer caused the temperature to fall.

   C The sun rose.

   D Heat from the stove on which breakfast was cooked caused the temperature to rise.

42. What is a good explanation of why the hottest temperature of the day is around 4:00 P.M.?

   F Exhaust from cars in rush-hour traffic causes the temperature to peak around 4:00 P.M.

   G The moon rises at this time and reflects extra sunlight toward Earth.

   H The sun is at its highest point in the sky at this time.

   J The air started warming as soon as the sun came up and continued warming until it began to set.

EARTH SCIENCE

GO ON

DIAGNOSTIC TEST B, Part 1 *(continued)*

Directions: *Use the diagram to answer questions 43 and 44.*

North American Air Masses

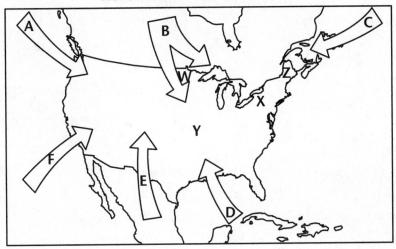

43. Describe the temperature and humidity of air mass A.

   A Cold and dry
   B Warm and moist
   C Cool and moist
   D Warm and dry

44. Which name would be given to air mass E?

   F Continental polar
   G Continental tropical
   H Maritime polar
   J Maritime tropical

Directions: *Use the diagram to answer questions 45 and 46.*

Local Winds

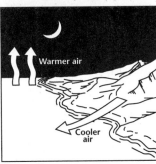

Diagram X

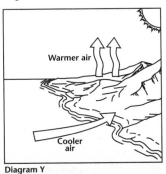

Diagram Y

45. Diagram X shows the formation of

   A a land breeze.
   B a sea breeze.
   C an off-shore breeze.
   D a night wind.

46. What is the main cause of the local winds shown in the diagram?

   F The different amounts of light cast by the sun and the moon
   G Water cooling faster than land
   H Unequal heating of land and water
   J Water heating faster than the land

EARTH SCIENCE

STOP

Directions: *Use the diagram to answer questions 47 and 48.*

Soil Development

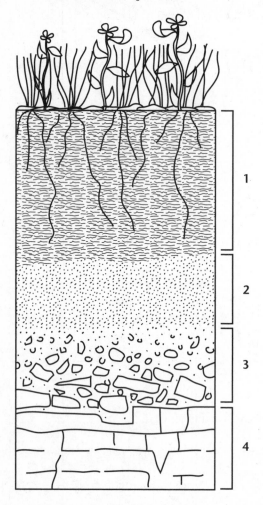

Directions: *Use the diagram to answer question 49.*

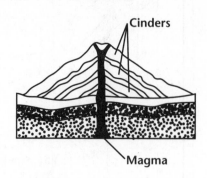

47. The layer of soil in which topsoil is found is

   A layer 1.   **C** layer 3.
   B layer 2.   **D** layer 4.

48. Layer 2 consists of

   F clay, minerals, and little humus.
   G humus only.
   H partly weathered rock.
   J topsoil.

49. The diagram shows the result when ash, cinders, and bombs build up in a steep pile around a volcano's vent. This type of volcano is a

   A cinder cone volcano.
   B shield volcano.
   C composite volcano.
   D dormant volcano.

50. The processes that break apart rock and soil and move them from one place to another are called

   F soil erosion and conservation.
   G weathering and erosion.
   H abrasion.
   J erosion and deposition.

51. Forces that shape Earth's surface by building up mountains and landmasses are called

   A constructive forces.
   B temperature and pressure.
   C destructive forces.
   D seismic waves.

GO ON

DIAGNOSTIC TEST B, Part 2 *(continued)*

Directions: Use the diagram to answer
questions 52 through 54.

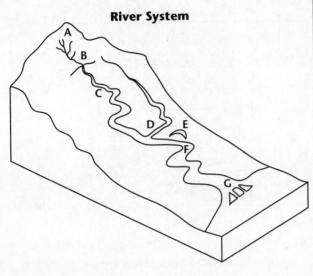

River System

52. Where is the water flowing fastest?

   F A and B   **H** E and F
   G C and D   **J** G

53. The water slows as it reaches letter G. What
feature forms just below letter G?

   A A meander
   B A delta
   C An oxbow lake
   D A rejuvenated stream

54. Below letter D, the area surrounding the river
is broad and flat. This area is called

   F a coastal plain
   G a delta.
   H a flood plain.
   J an estuary.

55. The agent of mechanical weathering in which
rock is worn away by the grinding action of
other rock particles is called

   A erosion.
   B cracking and peeling.
   C abrasion.
   D ice wedging.

Directions: Use the diagram to answer
question 56.

Slow constant force → **Rock Layers** ← Slow constant force

56. The diagram shows forces being applied to
rock layers. Which landform will result as the
forces are applied?

   F A dip or valley
   G A strike-slip fault
   H A crevasse or canyon
   J A mountain or buckling of rock layers

57. The law of superposition states that, in horizontal layers of sedimentary rock, each layer
is

   A younger than the layer above it and
older than the layer below it.
   B neither older nor younger than the
other layers.
   C older than the layer above it and
younger than the layer below it.
   D always older than any vertical layers.

GO ON

DIAGNOSTIC TEST B, Part 2 *(continued)*

Directions: *Use the diagram to answer question 58.*

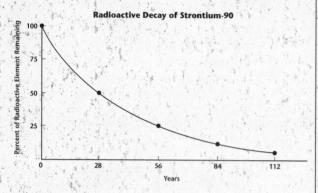

Radioactive Decay of Strontium-90

Directions: *Use the diagram to answer questions 61 and 62.*

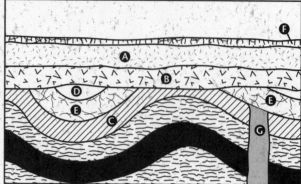

Rock Layers

58. Strontium-90 is a radioactive form of the element strontium that undergoes radioactive decay. The graph shows the decay of strontium-90 over time. What is the half-life of strontium-90?

F 25 years   **H** 50 years
G 28 years   **J** 56 years

59. The relative age of a rock is

A its age compared with the ages of other rocks.
B less than the age of the fossils the rock contains.
C the number of years since the rock formed.
D its age based on how much carbon-14 the rock contains.

60. The geologic time scale is a record of

F the thickness of sedimentary rock layers.
G the rate of fossil formation.
H the life forms and geologic events in Earth's history.
J the time since the extinction of dinosaurs.

61. What is the age of intrusion G in relation to the sedimentary rock layers through which it passes?

A Intrusion G is older than the rocks through which it passes.
B Intrusion G is the same age as the rocks through which it passes.
C Intrusion G is younger than the rocks through which it passes.
D Intrusion G may be older or younger than the rocks through which it passes.

62. If rock layers between B and D have eroded away, what is the boundary between B and D called?

F An intrusion
G An unconformity
H A strike-slip fault
J A reverse fault

63. Radioactive dating enables geologists to determine

A the age of the atoms in a rock.
B the half-life of a fossil organism.
C the relative ages of rocks.
D the absolute ages of rocks.

EARTH SCIENCE

GO ON

DIAGNOSTIC TEST B, Part 2 *(continued)*

Directions: *Use the diagram to answer questions 64 and 65.*

Location of Volcanoes

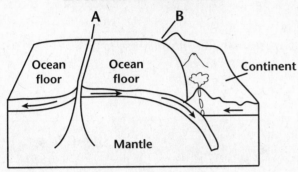

64. Which type of plate boundary is shown at B?

 F Convergent boundary
 G Divergent boundary
 H Transform fault boundary
 J Fractured boundary

65. Earthquakes would most likely occur

 A along the boundary marked A, where plates are moving apart.
 B along the boundary marked A, where plates are moving together.
 C along the boundary marked B, where plates are moving together.
 D along the boundary marked B, where plates are sliding past each other.

66. The process by which the ocean floor sinks beneath a deep-ocean trench and back into the mantle is known as

 F convection.
 G continental drift.
 H subduction.
 J conduction.

67. The geological theory that states that pieces of Earth's lithosphere are in constant, slow motion is the theory of

 A subduction.
 B plate tectonics.
 C sea-floor spreading.
 D deep-ocean trenches.

68. Geologists know that wherever plate movement stores energy in the rock along faults,

 F earthquakes are not likely.
 G earthquakes are likely.
 H an earthquake is occurring.
 J an earthquake could never occur.

69. In the process of sea-floor spreading, where does molten material rise from the mantle and erupt?

 A Along the edges of all the continents
 B Along the mid-ocean ridge
 C In deep-ocean trenches
 D At the north and south poles

EARTH SCIENCE

GO ON

Name _____ Date _____ Class _____

DIAGNOSTIC TEST B, Part 2 *(continued)*

Directions: Use the chart to answer question 70.

Mohs Hardness Scale

Mineral	Hardness
Talc	1
Gypsum	2
Calcite	3
Fluorite	4
Apatite	5
Feldspar	6
Quartz	7
Topaz	8
Corundum	9
Diamond	10

70. Which minerals in the table will scratch quartz?

   F Talc, gypsum, and calcite
   G Fluorite, apatite, and feldspar
   H Topaz, corundum, and diamond
   J All of the minerals listed will scratch quartz.

71. Mica breaks apart in flat sheets. This mineral can be described as having _____ in one direction.

   A fracture
   B luster
   C cleavage
   D hardness

72. The color of a mineral's powder is called its

   F streak.   **H** density.
   G luster.   **J** hardness.

Directions: Use the diagram to answer questions 73 and 74.

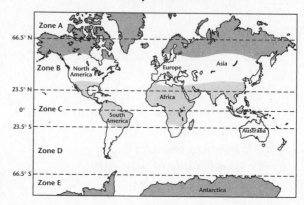

Temperature Zones

73. Scientists have divided Earth into several general climate zones. Most of the United States is in Zone B. This is a

   A polar zone.
   B temperate zone.
   C tropical zone.
   D equatorial zone.

74. The climate zones lying between 66.5° and 90° north and south latitude are called the

   F temperate zones.
   G polar zones.
   H tropical zones.
   J subtropical zones.

GO ON

EARTH SCIENCE

DIAGNOSTIC TEST B, Part 2 *(continued)*

75. The farther you live from the ocean, the more likely your climate will be a

  A marine climate.
  B tropical climate.
  C subtropical climate.
  D continental climate.

76. Jenna and Jack measured the temperature and humidity at different locations around their school building. They found that the area on the north side of the school is 5°F cooler and has a higher humidity than the area on the east side of the school. This is an example of

  F a microclimate.
  G a climate zone.
  H errors that can occur when reading a thermometer.
  J poor experimental design.

77. The two main factors that determine the climate of a region are

  A temperature and precipitation.
  B pressure and temperature.
  C altitude and pressure.
  D altitude and temperature.

78. There are many variations within each climate zone. The Great Plains east of the Rocky Mountains has a

  F temperate marine climate.
  G arid climate.
  H semiarid climate.
  J humid continental climate.

Directions: *Use the diagram to answer questions 79 and 80.*

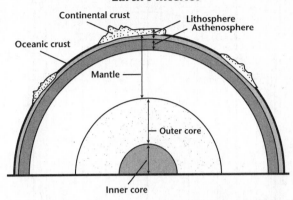

Earth's Interior

79. What is the correct order (starting from the surface) of Earth's layers?

  A Crust, outer core, inner core, mantle
  B Mantle, outer core, inner core, crust
  C Crust, mantle, outer core, inner core
  D Outer core, inner core, crust, mantle

80. Pressure increases with depth toward Earth's center. In which layer would you expect pressure to be the greatest?

  F Crust   **H** Outer core
  G Mantle   **J** Inner core

81. Most rocks formed on Earth's surface are

  A metamorphic rocks.
  B sedimentary rocks.
  C intrusive rocks.
  D igneous rocks.

EARTH SCIENCE

GO ON

DIAGNOSTIC TEST B, Part 2 *(continued)*

Directions: Use the diagram to answer questions 82 and 83.

The Rock Cycle

82. Rock that forms from the cooling of magma below the surface or lava at the surface is called

  F sedimentary rock.
  G metamorphic rock.
  H igneous rock.
  J coarse-grained rock.

83. Heat and pressure deep beneath Earth's surface can change any rock into

  A chemical rock.
  B gemstones.
  C metamorphic rock.
  D sedimentary rock.

84. The sedimentary rock formed when water deposits tiny particles of clay in very thin, flat layers is called

  F gypsum.
  G shale.
  H limestone.
  J calcite.

85. Which layer of Earth is made up partly of crust and partly of mantle material?

  A Asthenosphere   **C** Lithosphere
  B Crust   **D** Mantle

Directions: Use the diagram to answer questions 86 through 88.

Weather Map

86. What does A represent, and in what direction is it moving?

  F An unmoving stationary front
  G A cold front moving north
  H A warm front moving south
  J A cold front moving south

87. Line B connects points of equal temperature. What is it called?

  A An isotherm
  B A cold front
  C An isobar
  D A warm front

88. As D moves east, temperatures will

  F fall.   **H** stay the same.
  G rise.   **J** all be 50°F.

GO ON

Directions: Use the diagram to answer questions 89 through 91.

Topographic Map

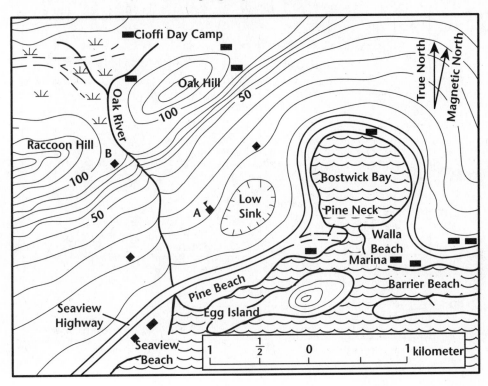

89. If elevation is shown in meters, what is the contour interval of the map?

A 5 meters   C 50 meters
B 10 meters   D 100 meters

90. At high tide during a coming storm, large waves are expected to wash up to the 10 m contour line. Which of the following will be flooded as a result?

F Cioffi Day Camp
G Raccoon Hill
H Oak Hill
J Walla Beach Marina

91. What is the difference in elevation between the school at point A and the house at point B?

A 35 meters   C 350 meters
B 70 meters   D 700 meters

EARTH SCIENCE

GO ON

DIAGNOSTIC TEST B, Part 2 *(continued)*

Directions: *Use the diagram to answer questions 92 and 93.*

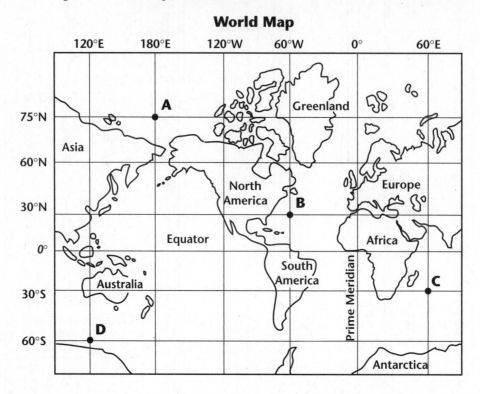

World Map

92. A ship is at Point C on the map. What is the exact position of the ship?

   F 30° S, 60° E
   G 30° N, 60° W
   H 60° S, 120° E
   J 75° N, 80° E

93. What is the difference in latitude, in degrees, between points A and D?

   A 75°   **C** 60°
   B 135°   **D** 180°

STOP

EARTH SCIENCE

DIAGNOSTIC TEST B, Part 3   EARTH SCIENCE

Directions: Read the passage, and then answer questions 94 through 96.

Using NASA Technology

You wouldn't wear the outer covering of an airplane to the swimming pool. You wouldn't wear moon boots to a track meet. Indirectly, though, these NASA creations have led to the development of quite a few items of clothing. NASA's Technology Transfer and Technology Spin-off programs encourage private enterprise to use and adapt space research for use in the public and commercial sectors.

The outer covering to an airplane? That technology, developed by NASA Langley Research Center, is riblets. These are small, barely visible grooves that were placed on the surface of an airplane to reduce surface friction and aerodynamic drag. Although the grooves are no deeper than a scratch, they make a surprising difference on the airflow near the plane's surface. Riblets are also featured on a line of competition swimsuits that in testing were found to bring competition results 10 to 15 percent faster than similar swimsuits.

Boots worn on the Moon needed to be specially cushioned because of the unusual lunar surface conditions. The material used has now turned up as a key element in a family of athletic shoes designed for improved shock absorption, energy return, and reduced foot fatigue. Tri-Lock® is the commercial incarnation of a three-dimensional space fabric. The design produces a system that retains shock-absorbing capabilities that stand up to the running, jumping, or pounding inflicted upon the shoe. The Earth-bound athletic shoes reduce impact forces that affect the muscular-skeletal system in the foot and lower leg, just like their Moon counterparts.

---

94. The use of space research in public and commercial applications

    F is illegal.
    G ended after the Apollo program.
    H produces few benefits to society.
    J is called technology transfer.

95. On airplanes, riblets

    A are added to the frame to increase the strength of the airplane in case of a crash.
    B are placed on the wing's surface to reduce friction and aerodynamic drag.
    C are offered as a dinner option on coast-to-coast flights.
    D provide added stability to the wings.

96. An advantage of the three-dimensional fabric being included in some athletic shoes is that

    F it makes the shoes waterproof.
    G it reduces the weight of the shoes.
    H it increases the shock-absorbing power of the shoe.
    J it allows the wearer to jump as high on Earth as the wearer would if on the moon.

EARTH SCIENCE

>GO ON>

DIAGNOSTIC TEST B, Part 3 *(continued)*

Directions: *Use the chart to answer questions 97 and 98.*

The Inner Planets

Planet	Diameter (km)	Period of Rotation (Earth days)	Average Distance From the Sun (km)	Period of Revolution (Earth years)
Mercury	4,878	59	58,000,000	0.24
Venus	12,104	243	108,000,000	0.62
Earth	12,756	1	150,000,000	1.0
Mars	6,794	1.03	228,000,000	1.9

97. What generalization can you make from the chart regarding the period of revolution of planets as you move farther from the sun?

  A The closer a planet is to the sun, the longer its period of revolution.

  B The farther a planet is from the sun, the longer its period of revolution.

  C The longer the period of rotation, the longer the period of revolution.

  D Distance from the sun has no effect on the period of revolution.

98. The diameter of Venus is to the diameter of Earth as the period of rotation of Earth is to the period of rotation of

  F Mercury.

  G Venus.

  H Mars.

  J Cannot be determined

99. The two factors that combine to keep the planets in orbit are

  A gravity and orbital speed.

  B orbital speed and mass.

  C mass and inertia.

  D gravity and inertia.

100. The asteroid belt is located

  F between Earth and Mars.

  G between Mars and Jupiter.

  H between Jupiter and Saturn.

  J between Saturn and Uranus.

101. Meteoroids usually come from

  A debris from other planets.

  B solar winds.

  C beyond the solar system.

  D comets or asteroids.

102. What do all of the inner planets have in common?

  F They have the same period of revolution.

  G They have the same period of rotation.

  H They have the same diameter.

  J They are small and have rocky surfaces.

103. An equinox occurs when

  A neither end of Earth's axis is tilted toward or away from the sun.

  B the north end of Earth's axis is tilted away from the sun.

  C the north end of Earth's axis is tilted toward the sun.

  D Earth's axis is parallel to the sun's rays.

EARTH SCIENCE

GO ON

DIAGNOSTIC TEST B, Part 3 *(continued)*

104. Day and night are caused by

    F   the tilt of Earth's axis.
    G   Earth's revolution around the sun.
    H   eclipses.
    J   Earth's rotation on its axis.

105. Alex worked in the garden for most of the day. He noticed that the length of his shadow changed with the sun's position in the sky. How did Alex's shadow appear around noontime?

    A   His shadow was long and stretched toward the western horizon.
    B   His shadow was long and stretched toward the eastern horizon.
    C   His shadow was very short.
    D   His shadow was medium in length and pointed due south.

106. In the Southern Hemisphere, the summer solstice occurs when the sun is directly overhead at

    F   the equator.
    G   23.5° south latitude.
    H   23.5° north latitude.
    J   30° south latitude.

107. Earth has seasons because

    A   Earth rotates on its axis.
    B   the distance between Earth and the sun changes.
    C   Earth's axis is tilted as it moves around the sun.
    D   the temperature of the sun changes.

108. One complete revolution of Earth around the sun takes about

    F   one rotation.   **H**   one year.
    G   one season.   **J**   one eclipse.

109. Earth's rotation takes about

    A   365 days.   **C**   24 hours.
    B   6 months.   **D**   1 month.

110. Fossil fuels are considered nonrenewable resources because they

    F   burn so quickly.
    G   are in such high demand.
    H   take hundreds of millions of years to form.
    J   pollute the air.

111. Solar cells are sometimes used to power all of the following **EXCEPT**

    A   calculators.
    B   lights.
    C   telephones.
    D   passenger trains.

112. Which of these is an example of a biomass fuel?

    F   Oil   **H**   Wood
    G   Natural gas   **J**   Coal

EARTH SCIENCE

DIAGNOSTIC TEST B, Part 3 *(continued)*

Directions: *Use the diagram to answer question 113.*

Types of Waste in a Sanitary Landfill

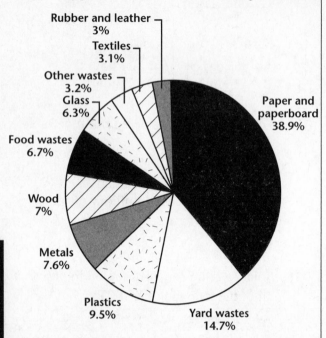

Rubber and leather
3%
Textiles
3.1%
Other wastes
3.2%
Glass
6.3%
Food wastes
6.7%
Wood
7%
Metals
7.6%
Plastics
9.5%
Yard wastes
14.7%
Paper and paperboard
38.9%

113. The Clark County commissioners want to reduce the amount of refuse sent to the local landfill. Which of the following suggestions has the potential to result in the greatest reduction of waste?

  A Recycling glass, plastic, and metals
  B Composting food wastes
  C Reusing rubber, leather, and textiles in new products
  D Recycling paper and paperboard

114. What is the most widely used source of renewable energy in the world today?

  F Hydroelectric power
  G Solar power
  H Biomass fuels
  J Tidal power

115. Wind energy is actually an indirect form of

  A electricity.
  B magnetic energy.
  C solar energy.
  D nuclear energy.

116. Energy conservation means

  F slowing down a chemical change.
  G burning a fuel to release energy.
  H using fossil fuels to produce electricity.
  J reducing energy use.

117. The Waste Recovery Company wants to build a landfill north of Tipp City. Which of these environmental factors should the local county commissioners investigate before they give the company a permit to build?

  A The direction of water drainage
  B The type of soil in the area
  C The depth of the water table
  D All of the above

118. The devices used in cars and trucks to reduce carbon monoxide emissions are called

  F mufflers.
  G catalytic converters.
  H scrubbers.
  J CFC substitutes.

119. Which of the following is a way to reduce water pollution?

  A Installing catalytic converters
  B Finding more CFC substitutes
  C Releasing more heated water from factories and power plants
  D Treating sewage before returning it to the environment

GO ON

EARTH SCIENCE

DIAGNOSTIC TEST B, Part 3 *(continued)*

120. What is the major source of photo-chemical smog?

   F Smoke from forest fires
   G CFCs and water vapor
   H Gases from volcanic eruptions
   J Gases emitted by automobiles and trucks

121. Increased amounts of carbon dioxide in Earth's atmosphere may lead to global warming. This, in turn, may lead to

   A more photochemical smog.
   B melting of the polar ice caps.
   C a hole in the ozone layer.
   D less of a greenhouse effect.

122. How can people help reduce the emissions that contribute to smog and the greenhouse effect?

   F By purchasing products that contain CFCs
   G By never pouring chemicals down the drain
   H By taking public transportation or walking instead of driving a car
   J By finding substitutes for garden chemicals

123. Which of the following is **NOT** a major source of freshwater pollution?

   A Human and animal wastes
   B Industrial wastes
   C Wetlands
   D Agricultural chemicals

Directions: *Use the diagram to answer questions 124 through 126.*

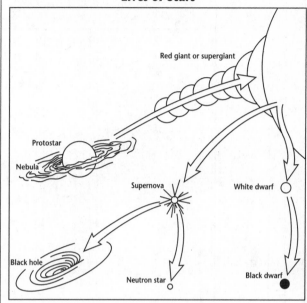

Lives of Stars

124. All stars begin their lives as parts of

   F nebulas.
   G protostars.
   H pulsars.
   J double stars.

125. When stars begin to run out of fuel, they first become

   A red giants or supergiants.
   B supernovas.
   C white dwarfs.
   D neutron stars.

126. The lifetime of a star depends on its

   F temperature.
   G brightness.
   H mass.
   J magnitude.

EARTH SCIENCE

GO ON

Name _____ Date _____ Class _____

DIAGNOSTIC TEST B, Part 3 *(continued)*

Directions: *Use the diagram to answer questions 127 through 129.*

Hertzsprung-Russell Diagram

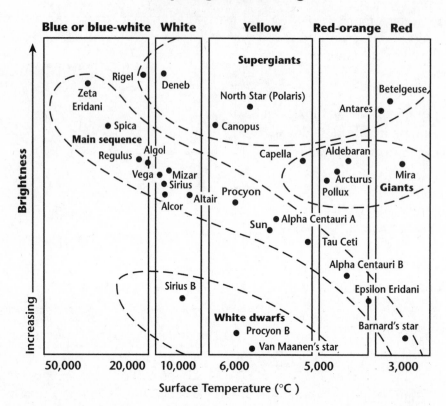

127. The sun is one of a group of stars called

   A the main sequence.

   B supergiants.

   C white dwarfs.

   D giants.

128. Jody used the diagram to compare our sun with Alpha Centauri A. Which statement best describes her conclusion?

   F Alpha Centauri A is slightly cooler and slightly brighter than our sun.

   G Our sun is slightly cooler and slightly brighter than Alpha Centauri A.

   H Alpha Centauri A and our sun are exactly alike.

   J Our sun is hotter and brighter than Alpha Centauri A.

129. Where are the coolest, dimmest stars found on the diagram?

   A In the upper left-hand corner near Zeta Eridani

   B In the center of the diagram near Procyon

   C Anywhere along the main sequence

   D In the lower right-hand corner near Barnard's star

130. During what phase can a lunar eclipse occur?

   F New moon   **H** Waxing gibbous

   G First quarter   **J** Full moon

DIAGNOSTIC TEST B, Part 3 *(continued)*

Directions: *Use the diagram to answer question 131.*

The Phases of the Moon

A   B   C   D

E   F   G   H

131. What is the correct order, starting with new moon, of the moon's phases?

A H, A, E, G, B, F, C, D
B H, A, B, G, E, F, C, D
C F, C, D, H, A, E, G, B
D B, F, C, D, H, A, E, G

132. When are tides highest?

F During the moon's first quarter phase
G When the sun, Earth, and the moon are nearly in a line
H During the moon's third quarter phase
J When the moon is at a right angle to the sun

133. Tides are caused mainly by

A Earth's rotation on its axis, which causes water to move.
B gravitational forces between the land and the water.
C strong winds blowing water onto coasts.
D differences in how much the moon and sun pull on different parts of Earth.

134. From new moon phase to full moon phase, you see

F an increasing amount of the lighted side of the moon.
G a decreasing amount of the lighted side of the moon.
H the same amount of the lighted side of the moon.
J more of the lighted side and then less of the lighted side of the moon.

135. For a solar eclipse to occur,

A the sun must be directly between Earth and the moon.
B the moon must be directly between Earth and the sun.
C the moon must be directly behind Earth.
D Earth must be directly between the sun and the moon.

EARTH SCIENCE

GO ON

DIAGNOSTIC TEST B, Part 3 *(continued)*

136. A light-year is

   F 365 days.

   G the distance light travels in a year.

   H the distance from Earth to Proxima Centauri.

   J the amount of light the sun produces in a year.

137. The distance from Earth to the sun is 150,000,000 kilometers. The distance from Earth to the star Proxima Centauri is approximately 4.2 light-years, or 40,000,000,000,000 kilometers (4.0×10^{13}). Why do scientists use the speed of light to describe distances between stars?

   A Light waves can be detected only from distant sources.

   B Telescopes can detect light-years more easily than kilometers.

   C The speed of light is more easily measured than the speed of sound.

   D Distances between some objects in the universe are too large to use kilometers.

138. How are elliptical galaxies and spiral galaxies different?

   F Elliptical galaxies have almost no gas or dust.

   G Elliptical galaxies vary more in shape than spiral galaxies.

   H Spiral galaxies have almost no gas or dust.

   J Spiral galaxies contain only old stars.

139. The most widely accepted theory that astronomers have developed to describe the formation of the universe is called the

   A expanding cloud theory.

   B time warp theory.

   C galactic expansion theory.

   D big-bang theory.

140. Scientists think that our universe is approximately

   F 1 to 5 million years old.

   G 1 to 2 billion years old.

   H 10 to 15 billion years old.

   J 100 to 200 billion years old.

141. The Milky Way Galaxy is a type of

   A spiral galaxy.

   B cloud galaxy.

   C elliptical galaxy.

   D irregular galaxy.

EARTH SCIENCE

GO ON

DIAGNOSTIC TEST B, Part 3 (continued)

Directions: Use the diagram to answer question 142.

Reflecting Telescope

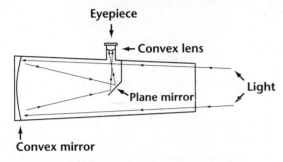

142. A reflecting telescope is designed to

   F break visible light into colors of the spectrum.

   G separate visible light from ultraviolet and radio waves.

   H gather and focus visible light.

   J work better with short-wavelength radiation.

143. Radio telescopes differ from optical telescopes in that they

   A collect and focus visible light.

   B collect and focus radio waves.

   C include an FM radio to which astronomers can listen while they scan the night skies.

   D must be placed in Earth orbit in order to function.

144. The chemical composition and temperature of a star can be determined using

   F a refracting telescope.

   G a spectrograph.

   H a satellite.

   J a reflecting telescope.

DIAGNOSTIC TEST A, Part 1   PHYSICAL SCIENCE

1. What is the first step of the scientific process?

   A Gather equipment for an experiment.
   B Plan an experiment.
   C Formulate a testable hypothesis.
   D Make a chart.

2. Elizabeth developed a hypothesis stating that people throw into the trash many materials that they could be recycling. Which investigative procedure should Elizabeth use to prove this hypothesis?

   F She should make a chart and list all of the materials that cannot be recycled.
   G She should collect specific data on the total number of items thrown into the trash during a given time period.
   H She should develop a detailed poster describing all of the types of items that can be recycled.
   J She should sort through items thrown away and collect data on how many of them can be recycled.

3. The purpose of repeated experimental trials is to

   A share the work.
   B provide practice.
   C validate conclusions.
   D supply data to record.

4. Jerome developed the following hypothesis for his science project:

   > The speed of a skateboard rolling downhill is greater on steep hills than on hills that are not steep.

   How can Jerome best test this hypothesis?

   F Push the skateboard with varying force down inclines set at different angles, and measure the force with which the skateboard hits the wall.
   G Push the skateboard with varying force down inclines set at different angles, and measure the distance traveled each time.
   H Roll the skateboard down an incline, and measure the force with which it hits the wall.
   J Roll the skateboard down inclines set at different angles, and measure the time it takes to roll the same distance each time.

5. Ian and Ron were making a model of a seesaw. They used weights to represent the people, a ruler to represent the seesaw, and a small piece of wood to represent the seesaw's fulcrum. What piece of scientific equipment should they use to measure force on the seesaw?

   A Stopwatch   C Meter stick
   B Spring scale   D Thermometer

PHYSICAL SCIENCE

⟩GO ON⟩

DIAGNOSTIC TEST A, Part 1 *(continued)*

6. Which of the following could you use most easily to determine the density of a liquid?

F

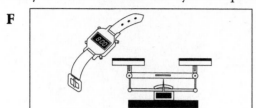

G

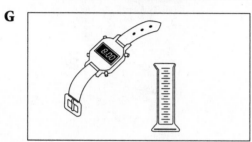

H

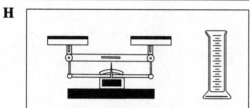

J

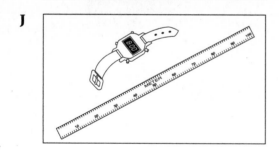

7. Erin has collected data on the time it takes waves to travel through water over various distances. She recorded her data in a table and now wants to display the data to make it easier to understand. Which graph should she use to display the data?

A Bar graph
B Site map
C Pie chart
D Line graph

Directions: *Use the chart to answer question 8.*

Race Times	
Raul	10.20 sec
Mark	10.22 sec
Tony	10.18 sec

8. Lydia helped as the timer in the school's track meet. The chart shows the results of a race she timed. Given this information, Lydia predicts that Tony will win the next race. From a scientific point of view, the major weakness of this prediction is that

F Lydia may like Tony better than the others.
G Lydia should have a better stopwatch.
H Lydia's prediction does not match the data.
J Lydia's data is not valid after only one trial.

⟩GO ON⟩

9. Bill put equal amounts of hot chocolate in three different containers: a foam cup, a ceramic mug, and a metal can. He measured the temperatures of the three samples of hot chocolate. They were all equal. Bill waited 15 minutes, and then he measured the temperatures again. The hot chocolate in the metal container had cooled the most. The hot chocolate in the foam cup had cooled the least. What should Bill conclude from this experiment?

A Metal is a good heat conductor, and foam is a good heat insulator.

B Foam is a heat conductor, and ceramic is the best heat insulator.

C Hot chocolate should never be consumed from a foam cup.

D Stirring hot chocolate causes it to cool more quickly.

Directions: Use the diagram to answer question 10.

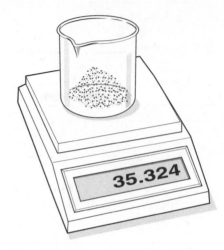

10. The beaker has a mass of 32.310 g. What is the mass of sodium bicarbonate in the beaker?

F 3.014 g   **H** 35.324 g

Directions: Use the diagram to answer question 11.

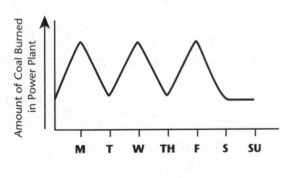

G 32.310 g   **J** 38.338 g

11. An area in the country has a coal-burning power plant. These diagrams were made from data collected there. What prediction can be made using the information in the diagrams?

A The acid in the rain will kill organisms.

B The acid in the rain will not rise until the following Monday.

C The acid in the rain will rise on Saturday after Friday's coal burning.

D The acid in the rain will rise suddenly on Friday because of coal-burning on that day.

GO ON

DIAGNOSTIC TEST A, Part 1 *(continued)*

Directions: *Use the diagram to answer question 12.*

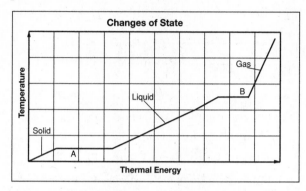

12. Which explanation is a reasonable interpretation of the data presented in this graph?

   F A gas contains more particles when it has less thermal energy.

   G A liquid changes state when it gains thermal energy.

   H All substances keep the same level of thermal energy with an increase in temperature.

   J A solid loses thermal energy as it reaches its melting point.

13. During Jack's laboratory investigation, he had to use a candle and matches. Which lab rule would be most important during this lab experiment?

   A Keep chemicals away from the eyes and skin.

   B Move electrical equipment away from the water.

   C Wash hands thoroughly with soap and water.

   D Tie back any loose hair and oversized clothing.

Directions: *Use the diagram to answer question 14.*

Safety Goggles   Electricity   Breakage   Sharp Objects (Scalpel)

14. The pictures shown are safety symbols used to warn students about potential hazards they may face while conducting a particular study. Which of the following would include all of these symbols?

   F An experiment with hydrochloric acid and sodium bicarbonate demonstrating chemical changes

   G An investigation into the speed of sound that measures the time it takes for each student to hear a sound

   H An activity that compares the illumination of light bulbs by cutting a hole in a shoebox and building a light tester.

   J A lab on waves during which students fill a pan with water and observe waves made by adding water droplets to it

15. During a laboratory experiment, a student accidentally spilled some hydrochloric acid onto his hand. The student should

   A neutralize the acid with salt.

   B rinse his hand with water.

   C immediately wipe up the spilled acid with a dry paper towel.

   D dilute the acid with vinegar.

16. The basic SI unit of length is the

   F meter.   **H** inch.

   G foot.   **J** mile.

PHYSICAL SCIENCE

> **GO ON**

DIAGNOSTIC TEST A, Part 1 *(continued)*

17. The density of a rock is 4.3 g/cm³. What is the density of the rock in kg/cm³?

   A   43 kg/cm³
   B   0.043 kg/cm³
   C   0.0043 kg/cm³
   D   0.00043 kg/cm³

18. Which would be the best unit of measurement for expressing the height of this candle?

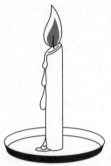

   F   Kilometers   **H**   Centimeters
   G   Meters   **J**   Millimeters

19. Gretchen's portable compact disc player always skips when someone bumps into her desk. She sees that it skips because it slides too easily on smooth surfaces. What could Gretchen do to solve the sliding problem?

   A   She could add a board to widen the area of her desk.
   B   She could add rubber circles to the bottom of the compact disc player.
   C   She could attach an adapter to allow her to plug the player into a wall socket.
   D   She could attach felt cushions to the bottoms of her desk's legs to keep the desk from rocking.

Directions: Use the diagram to answer question 20.

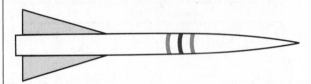

20. Supersonic planes fly faster than the speed of sound and cause a sonic boom that can damage buildings or break windows. Genevieve and Bo are trying to design a supersonic plane that will not cause a loud boom. They learned that planes with small, sharply angled wings produce softer booms. They made a model and used a computer simulator to test the size of the shock waves, which were very small. When they tried their model in a wind tunnel, they found that the plane would not fly. What design changes should they make so that their model will fly?

   F   They should give the plane larger wings and a shorter nose.
   G   They should build a longer plane body and smaller wings.
   H   They should attach the metal parts by welding instead of using rivets.
   J   They should use a heavier metal, such as steel, instead of aluminum.

PHYSICAL SCIENCE

>**GO ON**>

DIAGNOSTIC TEST A, Part 1 *(continued)*

21. What is the essential difference between natural quartz crystals and synthetic quartz crystals?

   A Natural quartz crystals are heavier than synthetic quartz crystals.

   B Natural quartz crystals occur in nature, and synthetic quartz crystals are made by people.

   C Natural quartz crystals are worth more than synthetic quartz crystals.

   D Natural quartz crystals are larger than synthetic quartz crystals.

Directions: Use the diagram to answer questions 22 and 23.

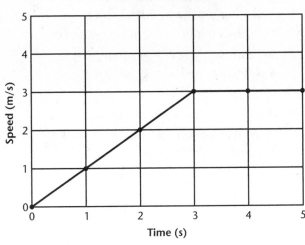

Speed of Ball Rolling Down a Ramp Onto Floor

22. What is the acceleration of the ball between 0 and 3 seconds?

   F 0 m/s^2 **H** 2 m/s^2
   G 1 m/s^2 **J** 3 m/s^2

23. If the ball had continued accelerating at the same rate, what would its speed have been after 4 seconds?

   A 0 m/s   **C** 4 m/s
   B 3 m/s   **D** 6 m/s

Directions: Use the diagram to answer question 24.

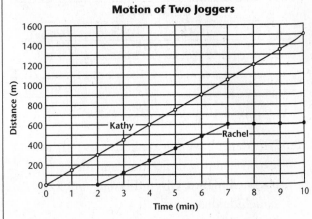

Motion of Two Joggers

24. If Kathy and Rachel started at the same place and followed the same course, after 5 minutes

   F they were at the same place.

   G Kathy was 375 m ahead of Rachel.

   H Kathy was 750 m ahead of Rachel.

   J Rachel was 375 m ahead of Kathy.

Directions: Use the chart to answer question 25.

Snail Travel

Minutes	Distance Traveled (cm)
1	0.76
2	1.10
3	1.40
4	1.52
5	1.54

25. Colleen used a ruler to measure the distance a snail traveled along the sidewalk. What was the snail's average speed for these five minutes?

   A 0.31 cm/min   **C** 0.76 cm/min

   B 0.70 cm/min   **D** 1.26 cm/min

PHYSICAL SCIENCE

GO ON

DIAGNOSTIC TEST A, Part 1 *(continued)*

Directions: Use the chart to answer questions 26 and 27.

Race Time			
Car	Track 1	Track 2	Track 3
1	2.0 s	2.3 s	4.0 s
2	2.5 s	3.0 s	4.5 s
3	4.0 s	4.6 s	8.0 s
4	1.5 s	2.0 s	3.5 s

26. The data above were collected as four toy cars rolled down race tracks made of inclined planes. Given this data, one can conclude that

F cars 1 and 2 are the fastest cars.
G car 3 is the heaviest car.
H track 3 is the longest track.
J track 2 is the shortest track.

27. If the cars were rolled down a fourth track, which car would probably finish first?

A Car 1   **C** Car 3
B Car 2   **D** Car 4

28. The rate at which velocity changes is called

F speed.   **H** acceleration.
G direction.   **J** motion.

29. If one of Earth's plates moves 5 centimeters every year, how far will it move in 500 years?

A 25 centimeters   **C** 250 meters
B 25 meters   **D** 25 kilometers

30. An object that is moving at constant speed will be accelerating if it is

F moving in a straight line.
G moving in a curved line.
H moving away from you.
J moving toward you.

31. When you are riding in a car and the car stops suddenly, you continue to move forward because of

A friction.   **C** inertia.
B gravity.   **D** centripetal force.

32. Ivan is doing an experiment with bowling balls. He sets four balls rolling at the same speed. Ball 1 has a mass of 9 kg, ball 2 has a mass of 8 kg, ball 3 has a mass of 5 kg, and ball 4 has a mass of 3 kg. Which ball will hit the bowling pins with the most force?

F Ball 1   **H** Ball 3
G Ball 2   **J** Ball 4

33. A girl jumps forward off a boat. According to Newton's third law of motion, what happens to the boat?

A The boat also moves forward.
B The boat remains motionless.
C The boat moves backward.
D The boat sinks.

PHYSICAL SCIENCE

>GO ON>

DIAGNOSTIC TEST A, Part 1 *(continued)*

Directions: Use the diagram to answer question 34.

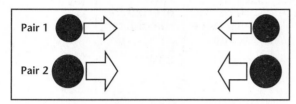

Assume that all of the objects in the diagram are solid and are made of the same material.

34. In this diagram,

   F the force of gravity is greater between the objects in Pair 1 than between the objects in Pair 2 because the objects in Pair 1 are closer together.

   G the force of gravity is greater between the objects in Pair 1 than between the objects in Pair 2 because the objects in Pair 1 have more mass.

   H the force of gravity is greater between the objects in Pair 2 than between the objects in Pair 1 because the objects in Pair 2 are closer together.

   J the force of gravity is greater between the objects in Pair 2 than between the objects in Pair 1 because the objects in Pair 2 have more mass.

35. Gillian attached a block to a spring scale and put the block on her desk. She pulled gently on the spring scale until the block just barely started moving. The spring scale read 15 N. Gillian had to use 15 N of force to overcome the force of

   A gravity.   **C** sliding friction.
   B static friction.   **D** momentum.

36. The force that keeps the electrons in an atom moving around the nucleus is

   F the strong nuclear force.
   G the weak nuclear force.
   H electromagnetic force.
   J gravity.

37. The product of an object's mass and velocity is called its

   A inertia.   **C** acceleration.
   B momentum.   **D** force.

38. According to the law of conservation of momentum, when two objects collide in the absence of friction,

   F velocity decreases.
   G velocity increases.
   H momentum is not lost.
   J only the object with the larger mass continues on.

39. If two balls collide with each other, they will move apart at the same speed if

   A they were traveling at the same speed when they hit and have the same mass.

   B they were traveling at the same speed when they hit.

   C they have the same mass.

   D they move apart at a right angle to each other.

40. Pressure is defined as

   F force per unit of time.
   G force per unit of area.
   H force per unit of mass.
   J force per unit of length.

PHYSICAL SCIENCE

GO ON

DIAGNOSTIC TEST A, Part 1 *(continued)*

Directions: *Use the chart to answer question 41.*

Object	Mass of the object	Length over which force is acting	Area of surface on which force is acting	Force exerted by the object
Picture hanging on a wall	9 kg	2.5 cm	1 cm²	88.2 N
Bowling ball on the floor	6 kg	1 cm	0.5 cm²	59 N
Box on a table	25 kg	35 cm	1,225 cm²	245 N
Person standing on a bridge	50 kg	35 cm	225 cm²	490 N

41. Which object listed above is exerting the greatest pressure?

   A The picture hanging on the wall
   B The bowling ball on the floor
   C The box on the table
   D The person on the bridge

42. Snowshoes help a person walk in deep snow by

   F decreasing the person's weight.
   G increasing the hardness of the snow.
   H decreasing the area over which the person's weight acts on the snow.
   J increasing the area over which the person's weight acts on the snow.

43. What scientific rule states that the pressure exerted by a moving stream of fluid is less than the pressure of the surrounding fluid?

   A Archimedes' principle
   B Pascal's principle
   C Bernoulli's principle
   D Newton's third law of motion

Directions: *Use the diagram to answer question 44.*

Blocks in Liquids

Identical wooden blocks

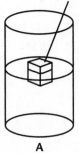 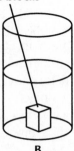

A   B

44. According to Archimedes' principle, the buoyant force in container A is

   F greater than the buoyant force in container B.
   G the same as the buoyant force in container B.
   H less than the buoyant force in container B.
   J zero.

45. What does a hydraulic system do?

   A Decrease pressure
   B Increase velocity
   C Multiply force
   D Reduce inertia

PHYSICAL SCIENCE

46. A ramp is an example of a simple machine called

   F an inclined plane.
   G a wedge.
   H a lever.
   J a pulley.

47. The ideal mechanical advantage of a wheel and axle is equal to the

   A radius of the wheel divided by the radius of the axle.
   B radius of the axle divided by the radius of the wheel.
   C radius of the wheel divided by the length of the axle.
   D length of the axle divided by the radius of the wheel.

48. What do machines do?

   F Change the amount of force you exert or the distance over which you exert the force
   G Increase the amount of work that is done
   H Decrease the amount of work that is done
   J Eliminate friction

49. Power equals work divided by

   A energy.   **C** force.
   B time.   **D** velocity.

50. Bart and Richie unloaded books from boxes on the floor and put them on shelves 1 m above the floor. Bart unloaded 20 kg of books in 10 min, and Richie unloaded 20 kg of books in 20 min. Which of the following statements is true?

   F Bart did more work and used more power than Richie.
   G Bart did more work than Richie, but Bart and Richie used the same amount of power.
   H Bart and Richie did the same amount of work and used the same amount of power.
   J Bart and Richie did the same amount of work, but Bart used more power.

51. Which of these is an example of work being done?

   A Holding a heavy piece of wood at a construction site
   B Trying to push a car that doesn't move out of deep snow
   C Pushing a child on a swing
   D Holding a door shut on a windy day so that it doesn't blow open

PHYSICAL SCIENCE

GO ON

DIAGNOSTIC TEST A, Part 2 (continued)

Directions: *Use the diagram to answer questions 52 and 53.*

Potential and Kinetic Energy

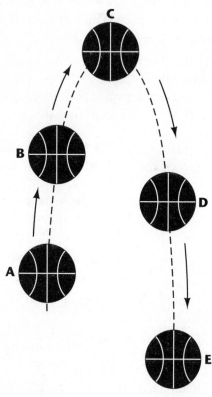

52. Which letter represents the position at which the basketball has the greatest potential energy?

F   A   H   C
G   B   J   D

53. According to the law of conservation of energy, if there is no air resistance, the total energy of this ball is

A   greatest when it starts to travel up.
B   greatest when it reaches the highest point of its path.
C   greatest when it hits the ground.
D   the same throughout its path.

54. When you rub your hands together on a cold day, you use friction to convert

F   mechanical energy into thermal energy.
G   thermal energy into nuclear energy.
H   nuclear energy into electrical energy.
J   electrical energy into electromagnetic energy.

55. When fossil fuels are burned to generate electricity, less than 50 percent of the energy in the fuel is converted to electrical energy. The rest of the energy is

A   used to run the power plant.
B   destroyed.
C   converted to matter.
D   converted to unusable forms such as heat.

56. Moving water can be used to produce electricity because

F   most forms of energy can be converted into other forms.
G   energy cannot be converted into other forms of energy.
H   potential energy can be converted into kinetic energy, but not vice versa.
J   kinetic energy can be converted into potential energy, but not vice versa.

57. The type of energy stored by fossil fuels such as coal is

A   kinetic energy.
B   mechanical energy.
C   chemical potential energy.
D   electromechanical energy.

58. Waves are formed when a source of energy causes a medium to

F   move.
G   compress.
H   expand.
J   vibrate.

GO ON

PHYSICAL SCIENCE

DIAGNOSTIC TEST A, Part 2 *(continued)*

Directions: *Use the diagram to answer question 59.*

Wave Generation

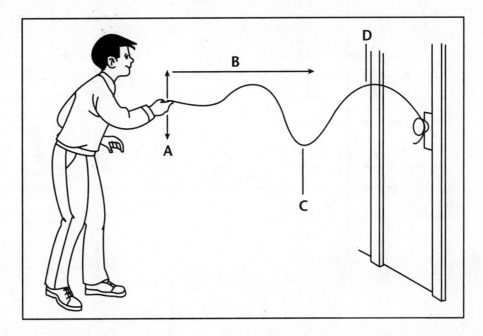

59. What kind of wave is being generated?

   A Longitudinal wave
   B Compressional wave
   C Transverse wave
   D Electromagnetic wave

60. The speed of a wave is its wavelength multiplied by its

   F amplitude.
   G vibration.
   H frequency.
   J reflection.

61. Niagara Falls is a good example of

   A kinetic energy being converted into potential energy.
   B potential energy being converted into kinetic energy.
   C energy being lost.
   D energy being created.

62. Kinetic energy increases as

   F mass increases and velocity decreases.
   G mass decreases and velocity increases.
   H both mass and velocity decrease.
   J both mass and velocity increase.

63. What type of energy does a spinning turbine have?

   A Electrical energy
   B Nuclear energy
   C Thermal energy
   D Mechanical energy

64. Electromagnetic waves can transfer energy without

   F a medium.
   G an electric field.
   H a magnetic field.
   J a change in either a magnetic or an electric field.

PHYSICAL SCIENCE

GO ON

DIAGNOSTIC TEST A, Part 2 *(continued)*

Directions: *Use the diagram to answer questions 65 and 66.*

Electromagnetic Spectrum

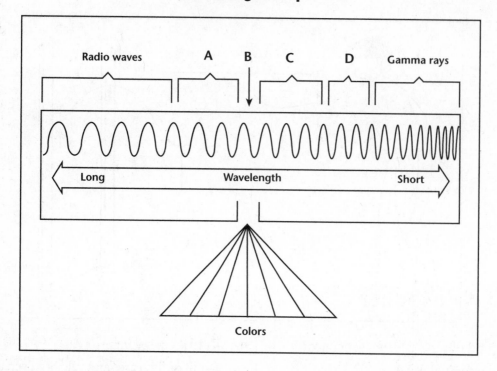

65. Which type of wave has the greatest energy?

   A Radio waves
   B Gamma rays
   C X-rays
   D Visible light

66. The electromagnetic waves with the highest frequencies are called

   F radio waves.
   G gamma rays.
   H X-rays.
   J visible light.

67. A laser beam can travel through a curled-up optical fiber because of

   A diffuse reflection.
   B holography.
   C total internal reflection.
   D regular reflection.

68. What happens when light passes from air into water?

   F The light speeds up.
   G The light continues at the same speed.
   H The light slows down.
   J The light forms a mirage

PHYSICAL SCIENCE

GO ON

Name _____   Date _____   Class _____

DIAGNOSTIC TEST A, Part 2 *(continued)*

Directions: *Use the diagram to answer question 69.*

Lens

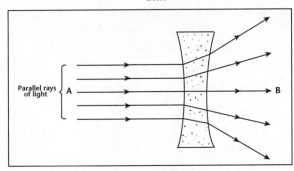

69. What type of image does this lens form?

   A A real image
   B A virtual image
   C An image that is smaller than the object
   D An image that is the same size as the original object

Directions: *Use the diagram to answer question 70.*

Reflection

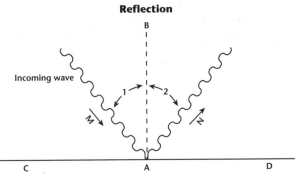

70. What do you know about angles 1 and 2?

   F Angle 1 is smaller than angle 2.
   G Angle 1 is larger than angle 2.
   H Angle 1 and angle 2 are the same size.
   J Angle 1 is 30°, and angle 2 is 60°.

Directions: *Use the diagram to answer question 71.*

Mirror

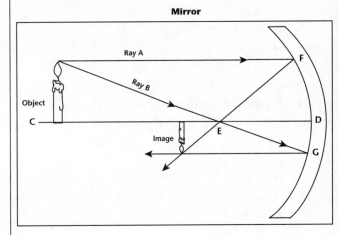

71. Relate the size and orientation of the image formed by the mirror to the size and orientation of the original object.

   A The image is the same size as the original object and is right-side up.
   B The image is the same size as the original object and is upside down.
   C The image is smaller than the original object and is right-side up.
   D The image is smaller than the original object and is upside down.

72. What occurs when parallel rays of light hit a rough or bumpy surface?

   F Regular reflection
   G Diffuse reflection
   H Refraction
   J Diffraction

PHYSICAL SCIENCE

DIAGNOSTIC TEST A, Part 2 *(continued)*

73. Visible light can be separated into the various colors of the visible spectrum by

   A a convex mirror.
   B a concave mirror.
   C a prism.
   D a polarizing filter.

74. A piece of cloth appears red under red light, green under green light, and blue under blue light. What color is the cloth?

   F Red
   G Green
   H Blue
   J White

75. Any two primary colors of light combined in equal amounts produce

   A a complementary color.
   B a secondary color.
   C a fluorescent color.
   D the third primary color.

76. Waves of which of the following colors of light have the highest frequency?

   F Red   **H** Green
   G Yellow   **J** Blue

77. As the mercury inside a thermometer heats up, the mercury

   A expands and moves higher in the tube.
   B contracts and moves lower in the tube.
   C reacts with the glass and turns red.
   D reacts with the glass and turns clear.

78. Heat, like work, is an energy transfer measured in

   F watts.   **H** joules.
   G degrees.   **J** kelvins.

79. Which of the following is true of the Celsius scale?

   A 212° is the boiling point of water.
   B 0° is absolute zero.
   C 0° is the freezing point of water.
   D 32° is the freezing point of water.

80. A measure of the average kinetic energy of the individual particles in an object is called

   F thermal energy.
   G conduction.
   H convection.
   J temperature.

PHYSICAL SCIENCE

>GO ON>

DIAGNOSTIC TEST A, Part 2 *(continued)*

Directions: Use the diagram to answer questions 81 though 83.

Thermos Bottle

- Cap
- Protective case
- Vacuum
- Double-walled glass bottle
- Air space
- Shock absorber

81. This bottle is designed to keep thermal energy from flowing in or out. Why does the bottle contain a vacuum, or space from which the air has been removed?

  A To prevent the loss of thermal energy by radiation

  B To prevent the loss of thermal energy by convection

  C To prevent the loss of thermal energy by conduction

  D To prevent the loss of thermal energy by induction

82. The glass walls of the device are covered with a shiny metallic coating. What type of transfer of thermal energy does the coating reduce?

  F Radiation   **H** Convection

  G Conduction   **J** Induction

83. The cap of this bottle is made of plastic. The use of plastic reduces the transfer of thermal energy into and out of this thermos bottle by

  A conduction.   **C** radiation.

  B convection.   **D** induction.

84. The buildup of charges on an object is called

  F static discharge.

  G static electricity.

  H positive charge.

  J negative charge.

85. Clothes in a dryer acquire static cling by

  A friction.

  B conduction.

  C induction.

  D static discharge.

PHYSICAL SCIENCE

GO ON

DIAGNOSTIC TEST A, Part 2 *(continued)*

Directions: Use the diagram to answer question 86.

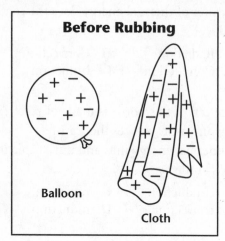

86. What is the overall electric charge on the balloon and on the cloth in the diagram?

F The balloon has a positive charge, and the cloth has a negative charge.

G The balloon has a negative charge, and the cloth has a negative charge.

H Both the balloon and the cloth have a positive charge.

J The balloon and the cloth are neutral.

87. During a thunderstorm, lightning strikes Earth when

A clouds have no charge.

B the static positive charge built up in the tops of clouds reunites with the static negative charge built up in the bottoms of clouds.

C a static negative charge builds up on Earth, inducing a static positive charge in the bottoms of clouds, and electrons flow from Earth to the clouds.

D the static negative charge built up in the bottoms of clouds induces a positive charge on Earth, and electrons flow from the clouds to Earth.

Directions: Use the diagram to answer question 88.

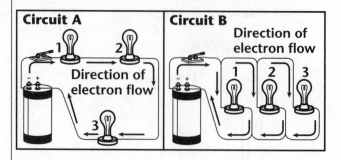

88. What will happen in Circuit A and Circuit B if bulb 1 in each circuit is removed?

F In both circuits, bulbs 2 and 3 will go out.

G In both circuits, bulbs 2 and 3 will remain lit.

H In Circuit A bulbs 2 and 3 will go out, and in Circuit B bulbs 2 and 3 will remain lit.

J In Circuit A bulbs 2 and 3 will remain lit, and in Circuit B bulbs 2 and 3 will go out.

89. In a series circuit with three bulbs,

A there are many paths for the current to take.

B the remaining two bulbs are not affected if one bulb burns out.

C all of the bulbs become dimmer as more bulbs are added.

D a switch is never used.

90. A connection that allows current to take an unintended path is called a

F short circuit.

G series circuit.

H parallel circuit.

J grounded circuit.

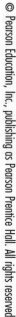

STOP

PHYSICAL SCIENCE

DIAGNOSTIC TEST A, Part 3   PHYSICAL SCIENCE

91. What happens when you break a magnet in half?

  A One half will have only a north pole, and the other half will have only a south pole.

  B Neither half will have a pole.

  C Each half will be a new magnet, with both a north and south pole.

  D Neither half will be able to attract or repel.

Directions: *Use the diagram to answer question 92.*

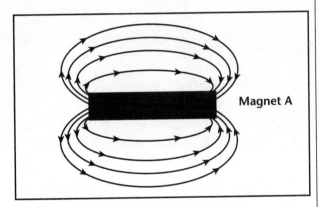

Magnet A

92. Study Magnet A. Where is the magnetic force the strongest on this bar magnet?

  F Near the north pole of the magnet

  G Near the middle of the magnet

  H At the magnet's north and south poles

  J Near the south pole of the magnet

93. The region around a magnet where the magnetic force is exerted is known as its

  A magnetic pole.

  B lodestone.

  C magnetic field.

  D magnetic domain.

94. An electric current produces

  F a magnetic domain.

  G a magnetic field.

  H an electrical resistance.

  J a permanent magnet.

95. When a current-carrying wire is placed in a magnetic field,

  A electrical energy is converted to mechanical energy.

  B mechanical energy is converted to electrical energy.

  C the wire becomes a permanent magnet.

  D the current stops flowing.

96. You can increase the strength of an electromagnet by

  F decreasing the current in the wire.

  G decreasing the number of loops in the wire.

  H using a stronger ferromagnetic material for the core.

  J increasing the thickness of the insulation on the wire.

97. In an electric motor,

  A a wire rotating in a magnetic field converts mechanical energy into electrical energy.

  B a magnet rotating in an electrical field converts mechanical energy into electrical energy.

  C a changing current of electricity flowing through a coil causes a magnet to rotate, converting electrical energy into mechanical energy.

  D a changing current of electricity flowing through a magnet converts electrical energy to mechanical energy.

PHYSICAL SCIENCE

GO ON

DIAGNOSTIC TEST A, Part 3 *(continued)*

98. The process of generating an electric current from the motion of a conductor in a magnetic field is

F conduction. **H** motion.
G induction. **J** magnetism.

Directions: *Use the diagram to answer question 99.*

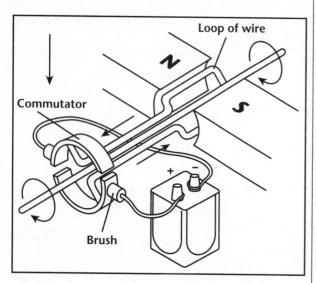

99. What common electrical device is shown in this diagram?

A Generator
B Electric motor
C Step-up transformer
D Step-down transformer

100. How is sound produced?

F By electromagnetic waves
G By making a material vibrate at a frequency that can be heard
H By causing the molecules in a solid to vibrate
J By pushing on a material

101. Sound waves are

A transverse waves.
B compressional waves.
C seismic waves.
D electromagnetic waves.

102. Sound does **NOT** travel through

F air.
G liquids.
H solids.
J outer space.

103. Why did Chuck Yeager's team choose a high altitude when trying to break the sound barrier?

A The temperature at high altitudes is lower, so sound travels faster.
B The temperature at high altitudes is lower, so sound travels more slowly.
C The temperature at high altitudes is higher, so sound travels faster.
D The temperature at high altitudes is higher, so sound travels more slowly.

GO ON

DIAGNOSTIC TEST A, Part 3 *(continued)*

Directions: Use the diagram to answer question 104.

Sonar

Ocean floor

104. Suppose that the sound waves of a sonar device on the ship are sent down and reflected back up by the sunken ship. If it takes 3 seconds for the waves to travel from their source to the sunken ship and back, what is the depth of the sunken ship? (Assume that the speed of the sound waves is 1,520 m/s.)

F 1,520 m
G 3,040 m
H 4,560 m
J 2,280 m

105. Which term refers to how high or low a sound seems to a person?

A Loudness
B Intensity
C Frequency
D Pitch

106. The pitch of a sound that you hear depends on the sound wave's

F loudness.
G frequency.
H intensity.
J speed.

107. Loudness, or sound level, is measured in units called

A decibels.
B hertz.
C meters per second.
D watts per square meter.

Directions: Use the diagram to answer question 108.

Sample Melting Points and Boiling Points

Substance	Melting Point (°C)	Boiling Point (°C)
Butane	−138	0
Methanol	−98	65
Heptane	−91	98
Iodine	114	184

108. Room temperature is approximately 20°C. Which substance in the table is a gas at room temperature?

F Butane
G Methanol
H Heptane
J Iodine

PHYSICAL SCIENCE

GO ON

DIAGNOSTIC TEST A, Part 3 *(continued)*

Directions: *Use the diagram to answer question 109.*

Solubilities of Various Compounds

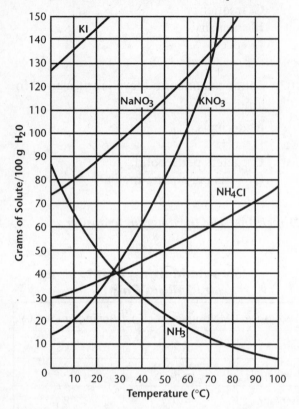

109. How many grams of potassium nitrate (KNO_3) will settle out when a saturated solution containing 100 grams of water is cooled from 70°C to 50°C?

    A 10 g   **C** 50 g
    B 25 g   **D** 70 g

110. Why do you need to know more than the melting point of a substance in order to accurately identify it?

    F The melting point of a substance changes over time.
    G Many substances have the same melting point.
    H All substances have the same melting point.
    J The melting point of a substance cannot be determined accurately.

111. Water vapor in the air turns to liquid water in the form of rain. This is an example of a

    A physical change.
    B chemical change.
    C chemical equation.
    D chemical formula.

112. When an inflated balloon is exposed to cold air,

    F the temperature inside the balloon rises.
    G the pressure inside the balloon rises.
    H the volume of the balloon increases.
    J the volume of the balloon decreases.

PHYSICAL SCIENCE

GO ON

DIAGNOSTIC TEST A, Part 3 *(continued)*

Directions: *Use the diagram to answer question 113.*

States of a Substance

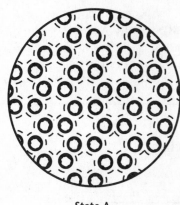 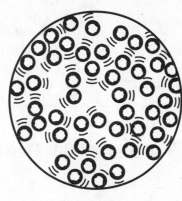 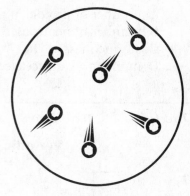

State A   State B   State C

113. Which of the states represents a liquid?

   A State A   **C** State C
   B State B   **D** States A and B

114. The largest particles inside the atom are

   F protons and electrons.
   G protons and neutrons.
   H neutrons and electrons.
   J electrons.

115. Atoms are electrically neutral because they have

   A equal numbers of protons and neutrons.
   B equal numbers of electrons and neutrons.
   C equal numbers of protons and electrons.
   D no charged particles.

116. According to the model of atoms we now use,

   F an atom cannot be broken down into smaller pieces.
   G an atom consists of a sphere of positive electricity in which negative electrons are embedded like raisins in a raisin muffin.
   H an atom consists of a nucleus of positive charge surrounded by electrons that orbit the nucleus in well-defined orbits.
   J an atom consists of a nucleus containing protons and neutrons. The nucleus is surrounded by electrons that move around the nucleus in orbitals defined by probability distributions.

117. A combination of two or more atoms that act as a single unit is called

   A an element.   **C** a molecule.
   B a compound.   **D** a solution.

118. Substances that **CANNOT** be broken down chemically into other substances are

   F elements.   **H** mixtures.
   G compounds.   **J** solutions.

PHYSICAL SCIENCE

GO ON

DIAGNOSTIC TEST A, Part 3 *(continued)*

119. The factor that has the greatest effect on how an atom interacts with other atoms is its

   A number of protons.
   B number of neutrons.
   C atomic mass.
   D number of valence electrons.

120. In an ionic bond, the valence electrons

   F are shared by two or more atoms.
   G are located on oppositely charged ions.
   H move easily around a lattice of positive ions.
   J are given off as beta particles.

Directions: Use the diagram to answer questions 121 through 123.

Periodic Table of the Elements (Top Section)

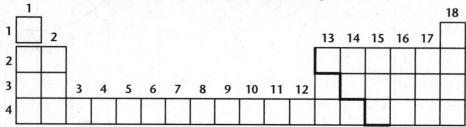

121. If a metal reacts violently with water, in which group is it likely to be found?

   A Group 1   **C** Group 17
   B Group 2   **D** Group 18

122. Where are nonmetals located on the periodic table?

   F To the left of the zigzag line
   G To the right of the zigzag line
   H In 3 and 4 rows
   J In Groups 1 through 4

123. Locate the box in Group 18 in the fourth period. Predict the state of matter and the chemical reactivity of the element that belongs in that box.

   A The element is a solid halogen that reacts easily with alkali metals.
   B The element is a gaseous halogen that reacts easily with alkaline earth metals.
   C The element is a noble gas that does not react easily with anything.
   D The element is a solid noble metal that does not react easily with anything.

PHYSICAL SCIENCE

>GO ON>

DIAGNOSTIC TEST A, Part 3 *(continued)*

124. What information in the periodic table indicates the number of protons in an atom?

    F The position of the element in its column

    G The element's chemical symbol

    H The element's atomic number

    J The element's atomic mass

125. As you move from Group 1 to Group 18 across a period of the periodic table,

    A the number of electrons in the outer shell increases.

    B the number of electrons in the outer shell decreases.

    C the number of electrons in the outer shell remains the same.

    D the number of protons in the nucleus decreases.

126. Atoms of elements in Group 1 of the periodic table react easily with atoms of elements in Group 17 because

    F atoms of elements in Group 1 each have one electron in their outer energy shells, and atoms of elements in Group 17 each have seven electrons in their outer energy shells.

    G atoms of elements in Group 1 each have seven electrons in their outer energy shells, and atoms of elements in Group 17 each have one electron in their outer energy shells.

    H atoms of elements in Group 1 each have two electrons in their outer energy shells, and atoms of elements in Group 17 each have eight electrons in their outer energy shells.

    J atoms of elements in Group 1 each have eight electrons in their outer energy shells, and atoms of elements in Group 17 each have two electrons in their outer energy shells.

127. A chemical reaction that absorbs energy in the form of heat will

    A go faster as temperature increases.

    B go more slowly as temperature increases.

    C be unaffected by temperature.

    D not occur.

128. The minimum amount of energy that has to be added to start a chemical reaction is the

    F exothermic energy.

    G endothermic energy.

    H activation energy.

    J chemical energy.

129. The only sure evidence for a chemical reaction is

    A the formation of a gas.

    B a color change.

    C the production of new materials.

    D changes in properties.

130. As the surface area of the reactants in a chemical reaction increases, the rate of the reaction

    F increases.

    G decreases.

    H remains the same.

    J increases and then decreases.

PHYSICAL SCIENCE

GO ON

DIAGNOSTIC TEST A, Part 3 *(continued)*

Directions: *Use the diagram to answer the questions 131 and 132.*

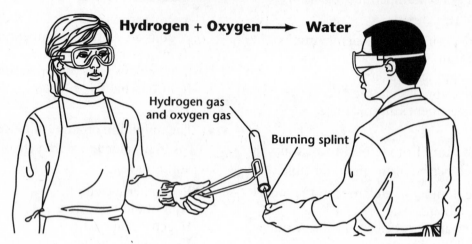

Hydrogen + Oxygen ⟶ Water

Hydrogen gas
and oxygen gas

Burning splint

131. Identify the reactant(s) and product(s) of this reaction.

   A The reactant is H_2O, and the products are H_2 and O_2.
   B The reactants are H_2 and O_2, and the product is H_2O.
   C The reactants are Hy and Ox, and the product is W.
   D The reactant is W, and the products are Hy and Ox.

132. In this reaction, how does the mass of the water formed in the reaction compare with the mass of the oxygen that reacts?

   F The mass of the water formed is greater than the mass of the oxygen that reacts.
   G The mass of the water formed is less than the mass of the oxygen that reacts.
   H The mass of the water formed is the same as the mass of the oxygen that reacts.
   J The mass of the water formed is half the mass of the oxygen that reacts.

133. In chemical reactions, what does the principle of conservation of mass mean?

   A Matter is not created or destroyed.
   B The total mass of the reactants is greater than the total mass of the products.
   C The total mass of the reactants is less than the total mass of the products.
   D Matter is not changed.

134. Which of the following is a balanced chemical equation?

   F $H_2O_2 \longrightarrow H_2O + O_2$
   G $2Fe_2O_3 + 3C \longrightarrow 4Fe + 3CO_2$
   H $SO_2 + O_2 + 2H_2O \longrightarrow 4H_2SO_4$
   J $2Mg + HCl \longrightarrow MgCl_2 + H_2$

135. A substance that tastes bitter, feels slippery, and turns red litmus paper blue is

   A an acid.   C an indicator.
   B a base.   D a solvent.

136. Any substance that forms hydrogen ions (H^+) in water is

   F an acid.   H an indicator.
   G a base.   J a salt.

PHYSICAL SCIENCE

> GO ON

DIAGNOSTIC TEST A, Part 3 *(continued)*

137. Neutralization is a reaction between

    A an acid and a base.
    B an acid and a metal.
    C a base and a salt.
    D a salt and water.

138. What does a neutralization reaction produce?

    F Acids
    G Bases
    H Water and a salt
    J Carbonated water

Directions: Use the diagram to answer questions 139 and 140.

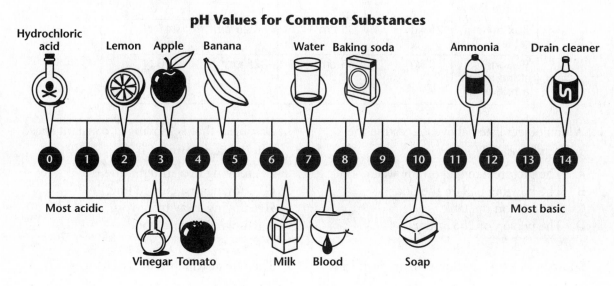

pH Values for Common Substances

139. What does the pH of drain cleaner tell you about the dangers of such a product?

    A It is a strong acid.
    B It is a weak acid.
    C It is a strong base.
    D It is a weak base.

140. Which pH indicates a neutral substance?

    F 0
    G 7
    H 10
    J 14

PHYSICAL SCIENCE

DIAGNOSTIC TEST B, Part 1   PHYSICAL SCIENCE

Directions: Use the chart to answer question 1.

Object	Mass of the object	Length over which force is acting	Area of surface on which force is acting	Force exerted by the object
Picture hanging on a wall	9 kg	2.5 cm	1 cm²	88.2 N
Bowling ball on the floor	6 kg	1 cm	0.5 cm²	59 N
Box on a table	25 kg	35 cm	1,225 cm²	245 N
Person standing on a bridge	50 kg	35 cm	225 cm²	490 N

1. Which object listed above is exerting the greatest pressure?

   A   The picture hanging on the wall
   B   The bowling ball on the floor
   C   The box on the table
   D   The person on the bridge

2. Snowshoes help a person walk in deep snow by

   F   decreasing the person's weight.
   G   increasing the hardness of the snow.
   H   decreasing the area over which the person's weight acts on the snow.
   J   increasing the area over which the person's weight acts on the snow.

3. Pressure is defined as

   A   force per unit of time.
   B   force per unit of area.
   C   force per unit of mass.
   D   force per unit of length.

4. An object that is moving at constant speed will be accelerating if it is

   F   moving in a straight line.
   G   moving in a curved line.
   H   moving away from you.
   J   moving toward you.

5. The rate at which velocity changes is called

   A   speed.   C   acceleration.
   B   direction.   D   motion.

6. If one of Earth's plates moves 5 centimeters every year, how far will it move in 500 years?

   F   25 centimeters   H   250 meters
   G   25 meters   J   25 kilometers

GO ON

PHYSICAL SCIENCE

DIAGNOSTIC TEST B, Part 1 *(continued)*

15. What scientific rule states that the pressure exerted by a moving stream of fluid is less than the pressure of the surrounding fluid?

A Archimedes' principle
B Pascal's principle
C Bernoulli's principle
D Newton's third law of motion

Directions: *Use the diagram to answer questions 16 and 17.*

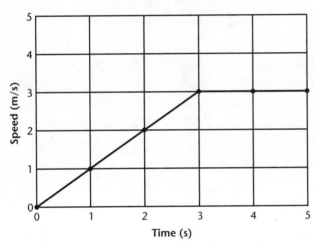

Speed of Ball Rolling Down a Ramp Onto Floor

16. What is the acceleration of the ball between 0 and 3 seconds?

F 0 m/s^2 **H** 2 m/s^2
G 1 m/s^2 **J** 3 m/s^2

17. If the ball had continued accelerating at the same rate, what would its speed have been after 4 seconds?

A 0 m/s   **C** 4 m/s
B 3 m/s   **D** 6 m/s

Directions: *Use the diagram to answer question 18.*

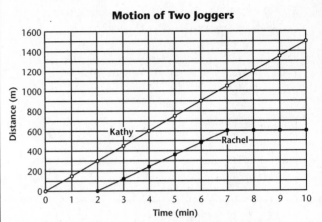

Motion of Two Joggers

18. If Kathy and Rachel started at the same place and followed the same course, after 5 minutes

F they were at the same place.
G Kathy was 375 m ahead of Rachel.
H Kathy was 750 m ahead of Rachel.
J Rachel was 375 m ahead of Kathy.

19. According to the law of conservation of momentum, when two objects collide in the absence of friction,

A velocity decreases.
B velocity increases.
C momentum is not lost.
D only the object with the larger mass continues on.

20. If two balls collide with each other, they will move apart at the same speed if

F they were traveling at the same speed when they hit and have the same mass.
G they were traveling at the same speed when they hit.
H they have the same mass.
J they move apart at a right angle to each other.

PHYSICAL SCIENCE

⟩GO ON⟩

DIAGNOSTIC TEST B, Part 1 *(continued)*

21. The product of an object's mass and velocity is called its

    A   inertia.   C   acceleration.
    B   momentum.   D   force.

Directions: *Use the diagram to answer question 22.*

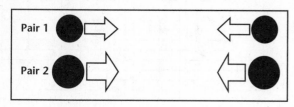

Assume that all of the objects in the diagram are solid and are made of the same material.

22. In this diagram,

    F   the force of gravity is greater between the objects in Pair 1 than between the objects in Pair 2 because the objects in Pair 1 are closer together.

    G   the force of gravity is greater between the objects in Pair 1 than between the objects in Pair 2 because the objects in Pair 1 have more mass.

    H   the force of gravity is greater between the objects in Pair 2 than between the objects in Pair 1 because the objects in Pair 2 are closer together.

    J   the force of gravity is greater between the objects in Pair 2 than between the objects in Pair 1 because the objects in Pair 2 have more mass.

23. The force that keeps the electrons in an atom moving around the nucleus is

    A   the strong nuclear force.
    B   the weak nuclear force.
    C   electromagnetic force.
    D   gravity.

24. Gillian attached a block to a spring scale and put the block on her desk. She pulled gently on the spring scale until the block just barely started moving. The spring scale read 15 N. Gillian had to use 15 N of force to overcome the force of

    F   gravity.   H   sliding friction.
    G   static friction.   J   momentum.

Directions: *Use the diagram to answer question 25.*

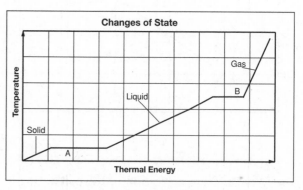

25. Which explanation is a reasonable interpretation of the data presented in this graph?

    A   A gas contains more particles when it has less thermal energy.

    B   A liquid changes state when it gains thermal energy.

    C   All substances keep the same level of thermal energy with an increase in temperature.

    D   A solid loses thermal energy as it reaches its melting point.

GO ON

PHYSICAL SCIENCE

DIAGNOSTIC TEST B, Part 1 *(continued)*

Directions: Use the diagram to answer question 26.

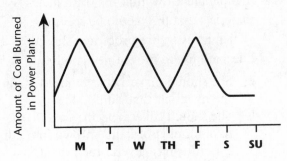

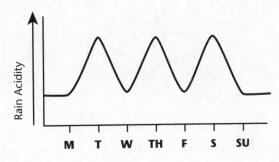

26. An area in the country has a coal-burning power plant. These diagrams were made from data collected there. What prediction can be made using the information in the diagrams?

   F The acid in the rain will kill organisms.
   G The acid in the rain will not rise until the following Monday.
   H The acid in the rain will rise on Saturday after Friday's coal burning.
   J The acid in the rain will rise suddenly on Friday because of coal-burning on that day.

27. Bill put equal amounts of hot chocolate in three different containers: a foam cup, a ceramic mug, and a metal can. He measured the temperatures of the three samples of hot chocolate. They were all equal. Bill waited 15 minutes, and then he measured the temperatures again. The hot chocolate in the metal container had cooled the most. The hot chocolate in the foam cup had cooled the least. What should Bill conclude from this experiment?

   A Metal is a good heat conductor, and foam is a good heat insulator.
   B Foam is a heat conductor, and ceramic is the best heat insulator.
   C Hot chocolate should never be consumed from a foam cup.
   D Stirring hot chocolate causes it to cool more quickly.

Directions: Use the diagram to answer question 28.

28. The beaker has a mass of 32.310 g. What is the mass of sodium bicarbonate in the beaker?

   F 3.014 g   **H** 35.324 g
   G 32.310 g   **J** 38.338 g

PHYSICAL SCIENCE

GO ON

DIAGNOSTIC TEST B, Part 1 (continued)

Directions: Use the chart to answer question 29.

Race Times	
Raul	10.20 sec
Mark	10.22 sec
Tony	10.18 sec

29. Lydia helped as the timer in the school's track meet. The chart shows the results of a race she timed. Given this information, Lydia predicts that Tony will win the next race. From a scientific point of view, the major weakness of this prediction is that

   A Lydia may like Tony better than the others.
   B Lydia should have a better stopwatch.
   C Lydia's prediction does not match the data.
   D Lydia's data is not valid after only one trial.

30. The purpose of repeated experimental trials is to

   F share the work.
   G provide practice.
   H validate conclusions.
   J supply data to record.

31. What is the first step of the scientific process?

   A Gather equipment for an experiment.
   B Plan an experiment.
   C Formulate a testable hypothesis.
   D Make a chart.

32. Elizabeth developed a hypothesis stating that people throw into the trash many materials that they could be recycling. Which investigative procedure should Elizabeth use to prove this hypothesis?

   F She should make a chart and list all of the materials that cannot be recycled.
   G She should collect specific data on the total number of items thrown into the trash during a given time period.
   H She should develop a detailed poster describing all of the types of items that can be recycled.
   J She should sort through items thrown away and collect data on how many of them can be recycled.

33. Jerome developed the following hypothesis for his science project:

   > The speed of a skateboard rolling downhill is greater on steep hills than on hills that are not steep.

   How can Jerome best test this hypothesis?

   A Push the skateboard with varying force down inclines set at different angles, and measure the force with which the skateboard hits the wall.
   B Push the skateboard with varying force down inclines set at different angles, and measure the distance traveled each time.
   C Roll the skateboard down an incline, and measure the force with which it hits the wall.
   D Roll the skateboard down inclines set at different angles, and measure the time it takes to roll the same distance each time.

PHYSICAL SCIENCE

DIAGNOSTIC TEST B, Part 1 *(continued)*

34. When you are riding in a car and the car stops suddenly, you continue to move forward because of

F friction. **H** inertia.
G gravity. **J** centripetal force.

35. Ivan is doing an experiment with bowling balls. He sets four balls rolling at the same speed. Ball 1 has a mass of 9 kg, ball 2 has a mass of 8 kg, ball 3 has a mass of 5 kg, and ball 4 has a mass of 3 kg. Which ball will hit the bowling pins with the most force?

A Ball 1 **C** Ball 3
B Ball 2 **D** Ball 4

36. A girl jumps forward off a boat. According to Newton's third law of motion, what happens to the boat?

F The boat also moves forward.
G The boat remains motionless.
H The boat moves backward.
J The boat sinks.

37. Erin has collected data on the time it takes waves to travel through water over various distances. She recorded her data in a table and now wants to display the data to make it easier to understand. Which graph should she use to display the data?

A Bar graph
B Site map
C Pie chart
D Line graph

38. Which of the following could you use most easily to determine the density of a liquid?

F
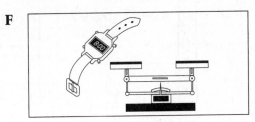

G
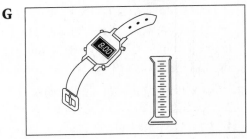

H
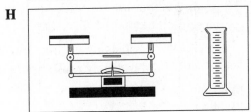

J
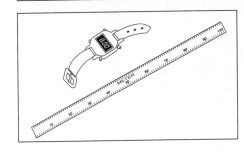

39. Ian and Ron were making a model of a seesaw. They used weights to represent the people, a ruler to represent the seesaw, and a small piece of wood to represent the seesaw's fulcrum. What piece of scientific equipment should they use to measure force on the seesaw?

A Stopwatch **C** Meter stick
B Spring scale **D** Thermometer

PHYSICAL SCIENCE

GO ON

DIAGNOSTIC TEST B, Part 1 *(continued)*

Directions: Use the chart to answer questions 40 and 41.

Race Time

Car	Track 1	Track 2	Track 3
1	2.0 s	2.3 s	4.0 s
2	2.5 s	3.0 s	4.5 s
3	4.0 s	4.6 s	8.0 s
4	1.5 s	2.0 s	3.5 s

40. The data above were collected as four toy cars rolled down race tracks made of inclined planes. Given this data, one can conclude that

F cars 1 and 2 are the fastest cars.
G car 3 is the heaviest car.
H track 3 is the longest track.
J track 2 is the shortest track.

41. If the cars were rolled down a fourth track, which car would probably finish first?

A Car 1   **C** Car 3
B Car 2   **D** Car 4

Directions: Use the chart to answer question 42.

Snail Travel

Minutes	Distance Traveled (cm)
1	0.76
2	1.10
3	1.40
4	1.52
5	1.54

42. Colleen used a ruler to measure the distance a snail traveled along the sidewalk. What was the snail's average speed for these five minutes?

F 0.31 cm/min   **H** 0.76 cm/min
G 0.70 cm/min   **J** 1.26 cm/min

43. The density of a rock is 4.3 g/cm^3. What is the density of the rock in kg/cm^3?

A 43 kg/cm^3
B 0.043 kg/cm^3
C 0.0043 kg/cm^3
D 0.00043 kg/cm^3

44. Which would be the best unit of measurement for expressing the height of this candle?

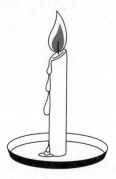

F Kilometers   **H** Centimeters
G Meters   **J** Millimeters

45. The basic SI unit of length is the

A meter.   **C** inch.
B foot.   **D** mile.

PHYSICAL SCIENCE

Directions: *Use the diagram to answer question 46.*

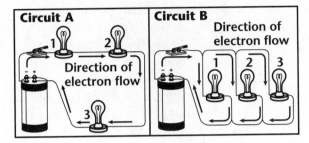

46. What will happen in Circuit A and Circuit B if bulb 1 in each circuit is removed?

   F In both circuits, bulbs 2 and 3 will go out.

   G In both circuits, bulbs 2 and 3 will remain lit.

   H In Circuit A bulbs 2 and 3 will go out, and in Circuit B bulbs 2 and 3 will remain lit.

   J In Circuit A bulbs 2 and 3 will remain lit, and in Circuit B bulbs 2 and 3 will go out.

47. In a series circuit with three bulbs,

   A there are many paths for the current to take.

   B the remaining two bulbs are not affected if one bulb burns out.

   C all of the bulbs become dimmer as more bulbs are added.

   D a switch is never used.

48. A connection that allows current to take an unintended path is called a

   F short circuit.

   G series circuit.

   H parallel circuit.

   J grounded circuit.

49. As the mercury inside a thermometer heats up, the mercury

   A expands and moves higher in the tube.

   B contracts and moves lower in the tube.

   C reacts with the glass and turns red.

   D reacts with the glass and turns clear.

50. Heat, like work, is an energy transfer measured in

   F watts.   **H** joules.

   G degrees.   **J** kelvins.

51. Which of the following is true of the Celsius scale?

   A 212° is the boiling point of water.

   B 0° is absolute zero.

   C 0° is the freezing point of water.

   D 32° is the freezing point of water.

52. A measure of the average kinetic energy of the individual particles in an object is called

   F thermal energy.

   G conduction.

   H convection.

   J temperature.

53. The buildup of charges on an object is called

   A static discharge.

   B static electricity.

   C positive charge.

   D negative charge.

PHYSICAL SCIENCE

GO ON

DIAGNOSTIC TEST B, Part 2 *(continued)*

54. Clothes in a dryer acquire static cling by

  F friction.
  G conduction.
  H induction.
  J static discharge.

Directions: Use the diagram to answer question 55.

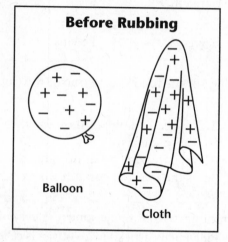

55. What is the overall electric charge on the balloon and on the cloth in the diagram?

  A The balloon has a positive charge, and the cloth has a negative charge.
  B The balloon has a negative charge, and the cloth has a negative charge.
  C Both the balloon and the cloth have a positive charge.
  D The balloon and the cloth are neutral.

56. During a thunderstorm, lightning strikes Earth when

  F clouds have no charge.
  G the static positive charge built up in the tops of clouds reunites with the static negative charge built up in the bottoms of clouds.
  H a static negative charge builds up on Earth, inducing a static positive charge in the bottoms of clouds, and electrons flow from Earth to the clouds.
  J the static negative charge built up in the bottoms of clouds induces a positive charge on Earth, and electrons flow from the clouds to Earth.

57. A piece of cloth appears red under red light, green under green light, and blue under blue light. What color is the cloth?

  A Red
  B Green
  C Blue
  D White

58. Waves of which of the following colors of light have the highest frequency?

  F Red   **H** Green
  G Yellow   **J** Blue

59. Any two primary colors of light combined in equal amounts produce

  A a complementary color.
  B a secondary color.
  C a fluorescent color.
  D the third primary color.

GO ON

PHYSICAL SCIENCE

DIAGNOSTIC TEST B, Part 2 *(continued)*

60. Visible light can be separated into the various colors of the visible spectrum by

   F a convex mirror.
   G a concave mirror.
   H a prism.
   J a polarizing filter.

61. When fossil fuels are burned to generate electricity, less than 50 percent of the energy in the fuel is converted to electrical energy. The rest of the energy is

   A used to run the power plant.
   B destroyed.
   C converted to matter.
   D converted to unusable forms such as heat.

62. Moving water can be used to produce electricity because

   F most forms of energy can be converted into other forms.
   G energy cannot be converted into other forms of energy.
   H potential energy can be converted into kinetic energy, but not vice versa.
   J kinetic energy can be converted into potential energy, but not vice versa.

63. The type of energy stored by fossil fuels such as coal is

   A kinetic energy.
   B mechanical energy.
   C chemical potential energy.
   D electromechanical energy.

64. When you rub your hands together on a cold day, you use friction to convert

   F mechanical energy into thermal energy.
   G thermal energy into nuclear energy.
   H nuclear energy into electrical energy.
   J electrical energy into electromagnetic energy.

Directions: *Use the diagram to answer questions 65 and 66.*

Potential and Kinetic Energy

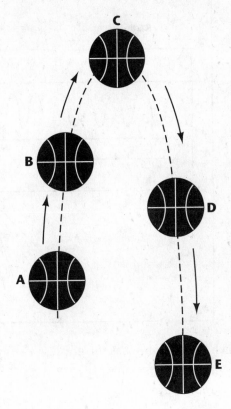

65. According to the law of conservation of energy, if there is no air resistance, the total energy of this ball is

   A greatest when it starts to travel up.
   B greatest when it reaches the highest point of its path.
   C greatest when it hits the ground.
   D the same throughout its path.

66. Which letter represents the position at which the basketball has the greatest potential energy?

   F A   **H** C
   G B   **J** D

PHYSICAL SCIENCE

GO ON

DIAGNOSTIC TEST B, Part 2 *(continued)*

Directions: *Use the diagram to answer questions 67 and 68.*

Electromagnetic Spectrum

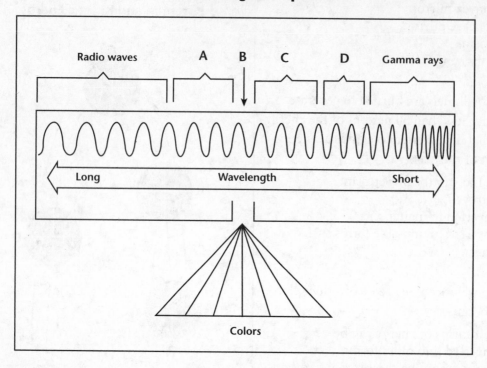

67. Which type of wave has the greatest energy?

   A Radio waves
   B Gamma rays
   C X-rays
   D Visible light

68. The electromagnetic waves with the highest frequencies are called

   F radio waves.
   G gamma rays.
   H X-rays.
   J visible light.

69. Electromagnetic waves can transfer energy without

   A a medium.
   B an electric field.
   C a magnetic field.
   D a change in either a magnetic or an electric field.

70. A ramp is an example of a simple machine called

   F an inclined plane.
   G a wedge.
   H a lever.
   J a pulley.

PHYSICAL SCIENCE

GO ON

DIAGNOSTIC TEST B, Part 2 (continued)

71. The ideal mechanical advantage of a wheel and axle is equal to the

   A radius of the wheel divided by the radius of the axle.

   B radius of the axle divided by the radius of the wheel.

   C radius of the wheel divided by the length of the axle.

   D length of the axle divided by the radius of the wheel.

72. What do machines do?

   F Change the amount of force you exert or the distance over which you exert the force

   G Increase the amount of work that is done

   H Decrease the amount of work that is done

   J Eliminate friction

73. Which of these is an example of work being done?

   A Holding a heavy piece of wood at a construction site

   B Trying to push a car that doesn't move out of deep snow

   C Pushing a child on a swing

   D Holding a door shut on a windy day so that it doesn't blow open

74. Power equals work divided by

   F energy.   **H** force.

   G time.   **J** velocity.

75. Bart and Richie unloaded books from boxes on the floor and put them on shelves 1 m above the floor. Bart unloaded 20 kg of books in 10 min, and Richie unloaded 20 kg of books in 20 min. Which of the following statements is true?

   A Bart did more work and used more power than Richie.

   B Bart did more work than Richie, but Bart and Richie used the same amount of power.

   C Bart and Richie did the same amount of work and used the same amount of power.

   D Bart and Richie did the same amount of work, but Bart used more power.

Directions: *Use the diagram to answer question 76.*

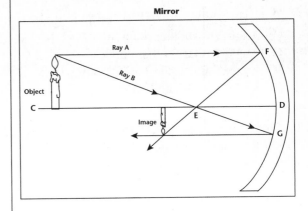

76. Relate the size and orientation of the image formed by the mirror to the size and orientation of the original object.

   F The image is the same size as the original object and is right-side up.

   G The image is the same size as the original object and is upside down.

   H The image is smaller than the original object and is right-side up.

   J The image is smaller than the original object and is upside down.

PHYSICAL SCIENCE

> GO ON

DIAGNOSTIC TEST B, Part 2 *(continued)*

77. What occurs when parallel rays of light hit a rough or bumpy surface?

   A Regular reflection
   B Diffuse reflection
   C Refraction
   D Diffraction

Directions: *Use the diagram to answer question 78.*

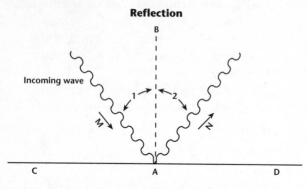

78. What do you know about angles 1 and 2?

   F Angle 1 is smaller than angle 2.
   G Angle 1 is larger than angle 2.
   H Angle 1 and angle 2 are the same size.
   J Angle 1 is 30°, and angle 2 is 60°.

79. A laser beam can travel through a curled-up optical fiber because of

   A diffuse reflection.
   B holography.
   C total internal reflection.
   D regular reflection.

80. What happens when light passes from air into water?

   F The light speeds up.
   G The light continues at the same speed.
   H The light slows down.
   J The light forms a mirage

Directions: *Use the diagram to answer question 81.*

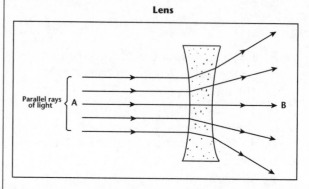

81. What type of image does this lens form?

   A A real image
   B A virtual image
   C An image that is smaller than the object
   D An image that is the same size as the original object

PHYSICAL SCIENCE

GO ON

DIAGNOSTIC TEST B, Part 2 *(continued)*

Directions: Use the diagram to answer questions 82 though 84.

Thermos Bottle

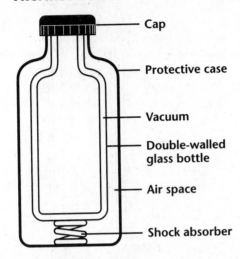

- Cap
- Protective case
- Vacuum
- Double-walled glass bottle
- Air space
- Shock absorber

82. This bottle is designed to keep thermal energy from flowing in or out. Why does the bottle contain a vacuum, or space from which the air has been removed?

  F To prevent the loss of thermal energy by radiation

  G To prevent the loss of thermal energy by convection

  H To prevent the loss of thermal energy by conduction

  J To prevent the loss of thermal energy by induction

83. The glass walls of the device are covered with a shiny metallic coating. What type of transfer of thermal energy does the coating reduce?

  A Radiation   **C** Convection

  B Conduction   **D** Induction

84. The cap of this bottle is made of plastic. The use of plastic reduces the transfer of thermal energy into and out of this thermos bottle by

  F conduction.   **H** radiation.

  G convection.   **J** induction.

85. What type of energy does a spinning turbine have?

  A Electrical energy

  B Nuclear energy

  C Thermal energy

  D Mechanical energy

86. Kinetic energy increases as

  F mass increases and velocity decreases.

  G mass decreases and velocity increases.

  H both mass and velocity decrease.

  J both mass and velocity increase.

87. Niagara Falls is a good example of

  A kinetic energy being converted into potential energy.

  B potential energy being converted into kinetic energy.

  C energy being lost.

  D energy being created.

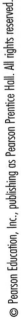

PHYSICAL SCIENCE

GO ON

DIAGNOSTIC TEST B, Part 2 *(continued)*

Directions: *Use the diagram to answer question 88.*

Wave Generation

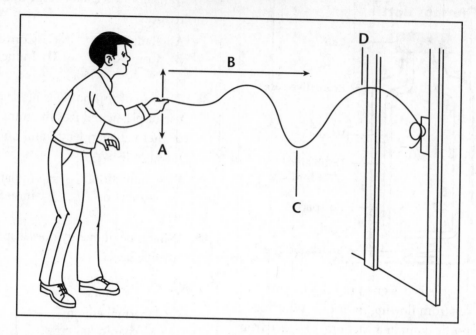

88. What kind of wave is being generated?

    F   Longitudinal wave
    G   Compressional wave
    H   Transverse wave
    J   Electromagnetic wave

89. The speed of a wave is its wavelength multiplied by its

    A   amplitude.
    B   vibration.
    C   frequency.
    D   reflection.

90. Waves are formed when a source of energy causes a medium to

    F   move.
    G   compress.
    H   expand.
    J   vibrate.

PHYSICAL SCIENCE

STOP

Name _____   Date _____   Class _____

Directions: *Use the diagram to answer questions 91 and 92.*

pH Values for Common Substances

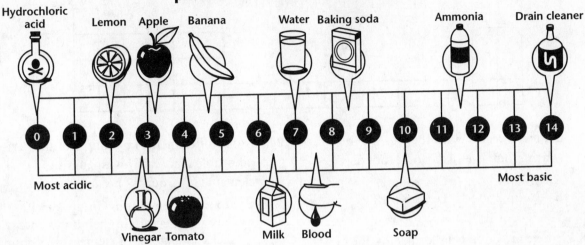

91. What does the pH of drain cleaner tell you about the dangers of such a product?

 A It is a strong acid.
 B It is a weak acid.
 C It is a strong base.
 D It is a weak base.

92. Which pH indicates a neutral substance?

 F 0
 G 7
 H 10
 J 14

93. Any substance that forms hydrogen ions (H⁺) in water is

 A an acid.   C an indicator.
 B a base.   D a salt.

94. What does a neutralization reaction produce?

 F Acids
 G Bases
 H Water and a salt
 J Carbonated water

95. Neutralization is a reaction between

 A an acid and a base.
 B an acid and a metal.
 C a base and a salt.
 D a salt and water.

96. A substance that tastes bitter, feels slippery, and turns red litmus paper blue is

 F an acid.   H an indicator.
 G a base.   J a solvent.

PHYSICAL SCIENCE

▷ **GO ON**

DIAGNOSTIC TEST B, Part 3 *(continued)*

Directions: *Use the diagram to answer questions 97 through 98.*

Periodic Table of the Elements (Top Section)

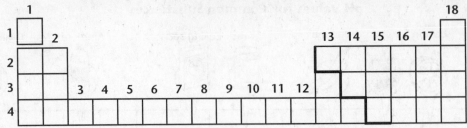

97. If a metal reacts violently with water, in which group is it likely to be found?

A Group 1   **C** Group 17
B Group 2   **D** Group 18

98. Where are nonmetals located on the periodic table?

F To the left of the zigzag line
G To the right of the zigzag line
H In 3 and 4 rows
J In Groups 1 through 4

99. Locate the box in Group 18 in the fourth period. Predict the state of matter and the chemical reactivity of the element that belongs in that box.

A The element is a solid halogen that reacts easily with alkali metals.
B The element is a gaseous halogen that reacts easily with alkaline earth metals.
C The element is a noble gas that does not react easily with anything.
D The element is a solid noble metal that does not react easily with anything.

100. Atoms of elements in Group 1 of the periodic table react easily with atoms of elements in Group 17 because

F atoms of elements in Group 1 each have one electron in their outer energy shells, and atoms of elements in Group 17 each have seven electrons in their outer energy shells.
G atoms of elements in Group 1 each have seven electrons in their outer energy shells, and atoms of elements in Group 17 each have one electron in their outer energy shells.
H atoms of elements in Group 1 each have two electrons in their outer energy shells, and atoms of elements in Group 17 each have eight electrons in their outer energy shells.
J atoms of elements in Group 1 each have eight electrons in their outer energy shells, and atoms of elements in Group 17 each have two electrons in their outer energy shells.

PHYSICAL SCIENCE

GO ON

DIAGNOSTIC TEST B, Part 3 *(continued)*

101. As you move from Group 1 to Group 18 across a period of the periodic table,

    A the number of electrons in the outer shell increases.

    B the number of electrons in the outer shell decreases.

    C the number of electrons in the outer shell remains the same.

    D the number of protons in the nucleus decreases.

102. What information in the periodic table indicates the number of protons in an atom?

    F The position of the element in its column

    G The element's chemical symbol

    H The element's atomic number

    J The element's atomic mass

Directions: Use the diagram to answer the questions 103 and 104.

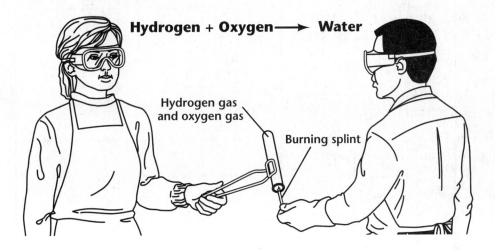

Hydrogen + Oxygen ⟶ Water

Hydrogen gas and oxygen gas

Burning splint

103. Identify the reactant(s) and product(s) of this reaction.

    A The reactant is H_2O, and the products are H_2 and O_2.

    B The reactants are H_2 and O_2, and the product is H_2O.

    C The reactants are Hy and Ox, and the product is W.

    D The reactant is W, and the products are Hy and Ox.

104. In this reaction, how does the mass of the water formed in the reaction compare with the mass of the oxygen that reacts?

    F The mass of the water formed is greater than the mass of the oxygen that reacts.

    G The mass of the water formed is less than the mass of the oxygen that reacts.

    H The mass of the water formed is the same as the mass of the oxygen that reacts.

    J The mass of the water formed is half the mass of the oxygen that reacts.

PHYSICAL SCIENCE

>GO ON>

DIAGNOSTIC TEST B, Part 3 *(continued)*

105. In chemical reactions, what does the principle of conservation of mass mean?

A Matter is not created or destroyed.

B The total mass of the reactants is greater than the total mass of the products.

C The total mass of the reactants is less than the total mass of the products.

D Matter is not changed.

106. Which of the following is a balanced chemical equation?

F $H_2O_2 \longrightarrow H_2O + O_2$

G $2Fe_2O_3 + 3C \longrightarrow 4Fe + 3CO_2$

H $SO_2 + O_2 + 2H_2O \longrightarrow 4H_2SO_4$

J $2Mg + HCl \longrightarrow MgCl_2 + H_2$

107. A combination of two or more atoms that act as a single unit is called

A an element.   **C** a molecule.

B a compound.   **D** a solution.

108. Substances that **CANNOT** be broken down chemically into other substances are

F elements.   **H** mixtures.

G compounds.   **J** solutions.

109. In an ionic bond, the valence electrons

A are shared by two or more atoms.

B are located on oppositely charged ions.

C move easily around a lattice of positive ions.

D are given off as beta particles.

110. The factor that has the greatest effect on how an atom interacts with other atoms is its

F number of protons.

G number of neutrons.

H atomic mass.

J number of valence electrons.

Directions: *Use the diagram to answer question 111.*

Sample Melting Points and Boiling Points

Substance	Melting Point (°C)	Boiling Point (°C)
Butane	−138	0
Methanol	−98	65
Heptane	−91	98
Iodine	114	184

111. Room temperature is approximately 20°C. Which substance in the table is a gas at room temperature?

A Butane

B Methanol

C Heptane

D Iodine

PHYSICAL SCIENCE

GO ON

DIAGNOSTIC TEST B, Part 3 *(continued)*

Directions: Use the diagram to answer question 112.

Solubilities of Various Compounds

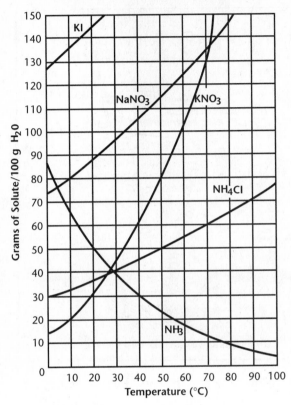

112. How many grams of potassium nitrate (KNO_3) will settle out when a saturated solution containing 100 grams of water is cooled from 70°C to 50°C?

   F 10 g   **H** 50 g
   G 25 g   **J** 70 g

113. Why do you need to know more than the melting point of a substance in order to accurately identify it?

   A The melting point of a substance changes over time.

   B Many substances have the same melting point.

   C All substances have the same melting point.

   D The melting point of a substance cannot be determined accurately.

114. According to the model of atoms we now use,

   F an atom cannot be broken down into smaller pieces.

   G an atom consists of a sphere of positive electricity in which negative electrons are embedded like raisins in a raisin muffin.

   H an atom consists of a nucleus of positive charge surrounded by electrons that orbit the nucleus in well-defined orbits.

   J an atom consists of a nucleus containing protons and neutrons. The nucleus is surrounded by electrons that move around the nucleus in orbitals defined by probability distributions.

115. The largest particles inside the atom are

   A protons and electrons.
   B protons and neutrons.
   C neutrons and electrons.
   D electrons.

116. Atoms are electrically neutral because they have

   F equal numbers of protons and neutrons.

   G equal numbers of electrons and neutrons.

   H equal numbers of protons and electrons.

   J no charged particles.

PHYSICAL SCIENCE

GO ON

DIAGNOSTIC TEST B, Part 3 *(continued)*

117. A chemical reaction that absorbs energy in the form of heat will

    A go faster as temperature increases.
    B go more slowly as temperature increases.
    C be unaffected by temperature.
    D not occur.

118. The minimum amount of energy that has to be added to start a chemical reaction is the

    F exothermic energy.
    G endothermic energy.
    H activation energy.
    J chemical energy.

119. The only sure evidence for a chemical reaction is

    A the formation of a gas.
    B a color change.
    C the production of new materials.
    D changes in properties.

120. As the surface area of the reactants in a chemical reaction increases, the rate of the reaction

    F increases.
    G decreases.
    H remains the same.
    J increases and then decreases.

Directions: Use the diagram to answer question 121.

Sonar

Ocean floor

121. Suppose that the sound waves of a sonar device on the ship are sent down and reflected back up by the sunken ship. If it takes 3 seconds for the waves to travel from their source to the sunken ship and back, what is the depth of the sunken ship? (Assume that the speed of the sound waves is 1,520 m/s.)

    A 1,520 m
    B 3,040 m
    C 4,560 m
    D 2,280 m

PHYSICAL SCIENCE

GO ON ▷

DIAGNOSTIC TEST B, Part 3 *(continued)*

122. Sound does **NOT** travel through

   F air.
   G liquids.
   H solids.
   J outer space.

123. Why did Chuck Yeager's team choose a high altitude when trying to break the sound barrier?

   A The temperature at high altitudes is lower, so sound travels faster.
   B The temperature at high altitudes is lower, so sound travels more slowly.
   C The temperature at high altitudes is higher, so sound travels faster.
   D The temperature at high altitudes is higher, so sound travels more slowly.

124. How is sound produced?

   F By electromagnetic waves
   G By making a material vibrate at a frequency that can be heard
   H By causing the molecules in a solid to vibrate
   J By pushing on a material

125. Sound waves are

   A transverse waves.
   B compressional waves.
   C seismic waves.
   D electromagnetic waves.

126. An electric current produces

   F a magnetic domain.
   G a magnetic field.
   H an electrical resistance.
   J a permanent magnet.

127. What happens when you break a magnet in half?

   A One half will have only a north pole, and the other half will have only a south pole.
   B Neither half will have a pole.
   C Each half will be a new magnet, with both a north and south pole.
   D Neither half will be able to attract or repel.

Directions: *Use the diagram to answer question 128.*

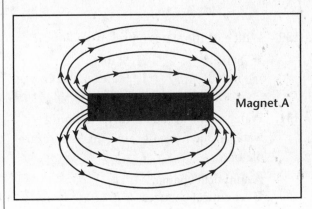

128. Study Magnet A. Where is the magnetic force the strongest on this bar magnet?

   F Near the north pole of the magnet
   G Near the middle of the magnet
   H At the magnet's north and south poles
   J Near the south pole of the magnet

129. The region around a magnet where the magnetic force is exerted is known as its

   A magnetic pole.
   B lodestone.
   C magnetic field.
   D magnetic domain.

PHYSICAL SCIENCE

GO ON

DIAGNOSTIC TEST B, Part 3 *(continued)*

Directions: *Use the diagram to answer question 130.*

States of a Substance

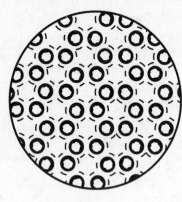

State A

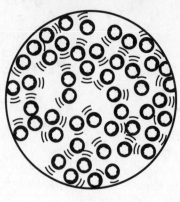

State B

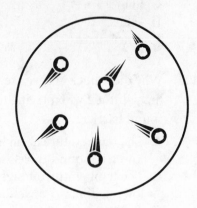

State C

130. Which of the states represents a liquid?

   F State A   **H** State C
   G State B   **J** States A and B

131. Water vapor in the air turns to liquid water in the form of rain. This is an example of a

   A physical change.
   B chemical change.
   C chemical equation.
   D chemical formula.

132. When an inflated balloon is exposed to cold air,

   F the temperature inside the balloon rises.
   G the pressure inside the balloon rises.
   H the volume of the balloon increases.
   J the volume of the balloon decreases.

133. Which term refers to how high or low a sound seems to a person?

   A Loudness
   B Intensity
   C Frequency
   D Pitch

134. The pitch of a sound that you hear depends on the sound wave's

   F loudness.
   G frequency.
   H intensity.
   J speed.

135. Loudness, or sound level, is measured in units called

   A decibels.
   B hertz.
   C meters per second.
   D watts per square meter.

PHYSICAL SCIENCE

GO ON

DIAGNOSTIC TEST B, Part 3 *(continued)*

136. The process of generating an electric current from the motion of a conductor in a magnetic field is

F conduction. H motion.

G induction. J magnetism.

Directions: *Use the diagram to answer question 137.*

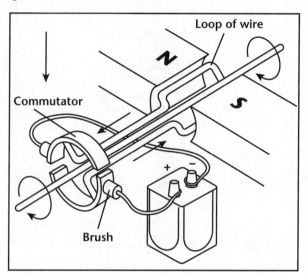

137. What common electrical device is shown in this diagram?

A Generator

B Electric motor

C Step-up transformer

D Step-down transformer

138. When a current-carrying wire is placed in a magnetic field,

F electrical energy is converted to mechanical energy.

G mechanical energy is converted to electrical energy.

H the wire becomes a permanent magnet.

J the current stops flowing.

139. You can increase the strength of an electromagnet by

A decreasing the current in the wire.

B decreasing the number of loops in the wire.

C using a stronger ferromagnetic material for the core.

D increasing the thickness of the insulation on the wire.

140. In an electric motor,

F a wire rotating in a magnetic field converts mechanical energy into electrical energy.

G a magnet rotating in an electrical field converts mechanical energy into electrical energy.

H a changing current of electricity flowing through a coil causes a magnet to rotate, converting electrical energy into mechanical energy.

J a changing current of electricity flowing through a magnet converts electrical energy to mechanical energy.

PHYSICAL SCIENCE

Screening Test, Part 1, Basic Process Skills

1. Ⓐ Ⓑ **Ⓒ** Ⓓ
2. Ⓐ Ⓑ **Ⓒ** Ⓓ
3. Ⓐ Ⓑ **Ⓒ** Ⓓ
4. Ⓐ Ⓑ Ⓒ **Ⓓ**
5. Ⓐ Ⓑ **Ⓒ** Ⓓ
6. **Ⓐ** Ⓑ Ⓒ Ⓓ
7. **Ⓐ** Ⓑ Ⓒ Ⓓ
8. Ⓐ Ⓑ Ⓒ **Ⓓ**
9. Ⓐ Ⓑ **Ⓒ** Ⓓ
10. Ⓐ Ⓑ **Ⓒ** Ⓓ
11. Ⓐ **Ⓑ** Ⓒ Ⓓ
12. Ⓐ **Ⓑ** Ⓒ Ⓓ

13. Ⓐ Ⓑ **Ⓒ** Ⓓ
14. Ⓐ **Ⓑ** Ⓒ Ⓓ
15. Ⓐ Ⓑ **Ⓒ** Ⓓ
16. **Ⓐ** Ⓑ Ⓒ Ⓓ
17. Ⓐ Ⓑ **Ⓒ** Ⓓ
18. **Ⓐ** Ⓑ Ⓒ Ⓓ
19. Ⓐ Ⓑ **Ⓒ** Ⓓ
20. Ⓐ Ⓑ **Ⓒ** Ⓓ
21. Ⓐ Ⓑ Ⓒ **Ⓓ**
22. Ⓐ **Ⓑ** Ⓒ Ⓓ
23. **Ⓐ** Ⓑ Ⓒ Ⓓ
24. Ⓐ **Ⓑ** Ⓒ Ⓓ

Screening Test, Part 2, Integrated Process Skills

1. Ⓐ **Ⓑ** Ⓒ Ⓓ
2. Ⓐ Ⓑ **Ⓒ** Ⓓ
3. Ⓐ Ⓑ Ⓒ **Ⓓ**
4. Ⓐ Ⓑ Ⓒ **Ⓓ**
5. Ⓐ **Ⓑ** Ⓒ Ⓓ
6. Ⓐ Ⓑ **Ⓒ** Ⓓ
7. **Ⓐ** Ⓑ Ⓒ Ⓓ
8. **Ⓐ** Ⓑ Ⓒ Ⓓ
9. **Ⓐ** Ⓑ Ⓒ Ⓓ
10. Ⓐ Ⓑ **Ⓒ** Ⓓ
11. Ⓐ **Ⓑ** Ⓒ Ⓓ

12. Ⓐ Ⓑ **Ⓒ** Ⓓ
13. Ⓐ Ⓑ **Ⓒ** Ⓓ
14. Ⓐ **Ⓑ** Ⓒ Ⓓ
15. Ⓐ **Ⓑ** Ⓒ Ⓓ
16. Ⓐ **Ⓑ** Ⓒ Ⓓ
17. Ⓐ **Ⓑ** Ⓒ Ⓓ
18. Ⓐ Ⓑ Ⓒ **Ⓓ**
19. Ⓐ **Ⓑ** Ⓒ Ⓓ
20. Ⓐ Ⓑ **Ⓒ** Ⓓ
21. **Ⓐ** Ⓑ Ⓒ Ⓓ

Screening Test, Part 3, Math Skills

1.	Ⓐ	Ⓑ	**Ⓒ**	Ⓓ		11.	Ⓐ	**Ⓑ**	Ⓒ	Ⓓ
2.	Ⓐ	Ⓑ	**Ⓒ**	Ⓓ		12.	Ⓐ	**Ⓑ**	Ⓒ	Ⓓ
3.	Ⓐ	Ⓑ	**Ⓒ**	Ⓓ		13.	Ⓐ	Ⓑ	**Ⓒ**	Ⓓ
4.	Ⓐ	Ⓑ	**Ⓒ**	Ⓓ		14.	Ⓐ	**Ⓑ**	Ⓒ	Ⓓ
5.	Ⓐ	**Ⓑ**	Ⓒ	Ⓓ		15.	**Ⓐ**	Ⓑ	Ⓒ	Ⓓ
6.	Ⓐ	Ⓑ	**Ⓒ**	Ⓓ		16.	**Ⓐ**	Ⓑ	Ⓒ	Ⓓ
7.	Ⓐ	Ⓑ	**Ⓒ**	Ⓓ		17.	Ⓐ	Ⓑ	Ⓒ	**Ⓓ**
8.	**Ⓐ**	Ⓑ	Ⓒ	Ⓓ		18.	**Ⓐ**	Ⓑ	Ⓒ	Ⓓ
9.	Ⓐ	Ⓑ	**Ⓒ**	Ⓓ		19.	**Ⓐ**	Ⓑ	Ⓒ	Ⓓ
10.	Ⓐ	**Ⓑ**	Ⓒ	Ⓓ		20.	Ⓐ	Ⓑ	**Ⓒ**	Ⓓ

Life Science Diagnostic Test A

1. B	**26.** H	**51.** B	**76.** G	**101.** A	**126.** F
2. J	**27.** A	**52.** F	**77.** B	**102.** G	**127.** B
3. D	**28.** J	**53.** C	**78.** F	**103.** B	**128.** J
4. F	**29.** D	**54.** G	**79.** D	**104.** H	**129.** A
5. D	**30.** J	**55.** B	**80.** H	**105.** C	**130.** F
6. G	**31.** B	**56.** G	**81.** D	**106.** G	**131.** D
7. D	**32.** J	**57.** A	**82.** J	**107.** B	**132.** F
8. J	**33.** D	**58.** F	**83.** B	**108.** J	**133.** B
9. A	**34.** F	**59.** C	**84.** H	**109.** B	**134.** H
10. J	**35.** B	**60.** J	**85.** C	**110.** F	**135.** C
11. B	**36.** J	**61.** C	**86.** F	**111.** B	**136.** J
12. H	**37.** B	**62.** J	**87.** D	**112.** F	**137.** D
13. B	**38.** H	**63.** D	**88.** J	**113.** D	**138.** J
14. H	**39.** B	**64.** H	**89.** A	**114.** H	**139.** B
15. D	**40.** H	**65.** A	**90.** H	**115.** B	**140.** G
16. H	**41.** C	**66.** G	**91.** A	**116.** G	**141.** A
17. D	**42.** F	**67.** B	**92.** G	**117.** A	**142.** G
18. H	**43.** B	**68.** F	**93.** D	**118.** H	**143.** D
19. B	**44.** F	**69.** A	**94.** G	**119.** D	**144.** G
20. G	**45.** B	**70.** F	**95.** D	**120.** H	
21. A	**46.** G	**71.** A	**96.** H	**121.** C	
22. H	**47.** C	**72.** H	**97.** A	**122.** J	
23. D	**48.** J	**73.** A	**98.** H	**123.** C	
24. G	**49.** A	**74.** H	**99.** D	**124.** G	
25. A	**50.** J	**75.** D	**100.** G	**125.** A	

ANSWER KEY

Life Science Diagnostic Test B

1. B	**26.** J	**51.** B	**76.** H	**101.** C	**126.** G
2. G	**27.** B	**52.** H	**77.** D	**102.** J	**127.** B
3. A	**28.** J	**53.** C	**78.** F	**103.** A	**128.** F
4. F	**29.** D	**54.** F	**79.** D	**104.** F	**129.** B
5. D	**30.** J	**55.** D	**80.** G	**105.** C	**130.** J
6. G	**31.** B	**56.** J	**81.** D	**106.** J	**131.** C
7. C	**32.** H	**57.** D	**82.** H	**107.** D	**132.** J
8. H	**33.** B	**58.** G	**83.** A	**108.** J	**133.** B
9. D	**34.** G	**59.** D	**84.** H	**109.** A	**134.** J
10. G	**35.** C	**60.** F	**85.** D	**110.** H	**135.** B
11. D	**36.** J	**61.** C	**86.** J	**111.** C	**136.** F
12. G	**37.** B	**62.** F	**87.** C	**112.** H	**137.** B
13. C	**38.** F	**63.** B	**88.** G	**113.** D	**138.** G
14. J	**39.** D	**64.** F	**89.** A	**114.** J	**139.** A
15. A	**40.** G	**65.** B	**90.** F	**115.** B	**140.** G
16. J	**41.** C	**66.** G	**91.** D	**116.** J	**141.** D
17. B	**42.** J	**67.** A	**92.** G	**117.** B	**142.** G
18. H	**43.** D	**68.** G	**93.** B	**118.** G	**143.** B
19. D	**44.** J	**69.** A	**94.** J	**119.** A	**144.** H
20. H	**45.** A	**70.** H	**95.** A	**120.** J	
21. A	**46.** J	**71.** B	**96.** H	**121.** B	
22. J	**47.** C	**72.** H	**97.** A	**122.** F	
23. D	**48.** F	**73.** A	**98.** H	**123.** A	
24. G	**49.** B	**74.** H	**99.** A	**124.** G	
25. A	**50.** F	**75.** D	**100.** G	**125.** C	

© Pearson Education, Inc., publishing as Pearson Prentice Hall. All rights reserved.

Name _____ Date _____ Class _____

LIFE SCIENCE

TESTS			Life Science Objectives	Question Numbers Test A	Question Numbers Test B	Number Correct	Proficient? Yes or No
SAT9	ITBS	TerraNova					
Topic: Scientific Inquiry/Process							
✓	✓		1 Understand the fundamental concepts of science inquiry.	1, 2, 3	27, 28, 29	□/6	
✓	✓		2 Demonstrate the ability to perform science inquiry. • Associate a scientific instrument with its use.	4, 5, 6	15, 16, 17	□/6	
✓	✓		3 Use the process skills of science. • Draw a conclusion from data. • Evaluate graphs of experimental data.	7, 8, 9	43, 44, 45	□/6	
	✓		4 Apply safety skills.	10, 11, 12	12, 13, 14	□/6	
	✓		5 Understand, use, and convert SI units.	13, 14, 15	34, 35, 36	□/6	
Topic: Personal and Social Perspectives in Science							
✓	✓		1 Demonstrate an understanding of the fundamental concepts and principles of science that have a direct impact on personal and social issues. • Personal health • Populations • Resources • Environment • Technology	16, 17, 18	18, 19, 20	□/6	
Topic: Living Things—Cells							
✓	✓		1 Describe cell structure and function. • Identify major parts of plant and animal cells. • Identify the functions of different types of cells. • Describe the movement of materials into and out of the cell for the maintenance of homeostasis.	19, 20, 21, 22, 23, 24, 25, 26	1, 2, 3, 4, 5, 6, 7, 8	□/16	
Topic: Living Things—Growth and Reproduction							
3	3	3	1 Understand how organisms grow. • Describe the process of mitosis. • Evaluate the design of an experiment about an organism's growth.	27, 28, 29	21, 22, 23	□/6	
3	3	3	2 Understand how organisms reproduce asexually. • Describe several methods of asexual reproduction. • Read a graph about organism reproduction.	30, 31, 32	9, 10, 11	□/6	

Name _____ Date _____ Class _____

| TESTS | | | Life Science Objectives *(continued)* | Question Numbers Test A | Question Numbers Test B | Number Correct | Proficient? Yes or No |
SAT9	ITBS	TerraNova					
✓	✓		3 Understand how organisms reproduce sexually. • Describe the process of meiosis. • Interpret information about the growth of an organism from a graph.	33, 34 35	24, 25, 26	□/6	

Topic: Living Things—Cells to Systems

| TESTS | | | Life Science Objectives *(continued)* | Question Numbers Test A | Question Numbers Test B | Number Correct | Proficient? Yes or No |
SAT9	ITBS	TerraNova					
✓	✓	✓	1 Identify how structure complements function at different levels of organization. • Describe the organization of cells into tissues, organs, and systems.	36, 37, 38, 39	30, 31, 32, 33	□/8	
✓	✓	✓	2 Identify and describe human body systems. • Identify and describe organs and their functions. • Describe interactions among human body systems.	40, 41, 42, 43, 44	46, 47, 48, 49, 50	□/10	
✓	✓		3 Identify the responses of organisms caused by internal or external stimuli. • Identify feedback mechanisms that maintain equilibrium of systems, such as body temperature and chemical reactions. • Identify responses in organisms to external stimuli such as the presence or absence of heat or light.	45, 46, 47, 48, 49, 50	37, 38, 39, 40, 41, 42	□/12	
✓	✓		4 Discuss the immune system and the ways in which humans augment this system. • Define the immune system, and describe how it defends the body against infectious diseases. • Identify how health care practices have decreased infectious disease. • Identify recent medical discoveries that improve the treatment of serious illnesses.	51, 52, 53, 54, 55, 56, 57, 58	64, 65, 66, 67, 68, 69, 70, 71	□/16	
✓			5 Explain the relationship between behavior and overall health. • Relate causes and effects of health problems. • Read a food product label. • Understand nutritional information.	59, 60, 61, 62	84, 85, 86, 87	□/8	

Name _____ Date _____ Class _____

LIFE SCIENCE

TESTS			Life Science Objectives *(continued)*	Question Numbers Test A	Question Numbers Test B	Number Correct	Proficient? Yes or No
SAT9	ITBS	TerraNova					
Topic: Genetics							
✓	✓		1 Understand that the instructions for traits are contained in the genetic material of the organism. • Identify that sexual reproduction results in more diverse offspring, and asexual reproduction results in more uniform offspring. • Identify the role of genes in inheritance.	63, 64, 65, 66	80, 81, 82, 83	□/8	
✓			2 Distinguish between dominant and recessive traits and recognize that inherited traits of an individual are contained in genetic material. • Predict the results of genetic crosses using a Punnet square. • Explain the use of a pedigree to trace a particular trait. • Describe how human traits are determined. • Describe common genetic disorders and how they can be inherited.	67, 68, 69, 70, 71, 72, 73, 74, 75, 76, 77	88, 89, 90, 91, 92, 93, 94, 95, 96, 97, 98	□/22	
✓			3 Identify that change in environmental conditions can affect the survival of individuals and of species. • Distinguish between inherited traits and other characteristics that result from interactions with the environment. • Identify changes in traits that can occur over several generations through natural occurrence and selective breeding. • Describe various advances due to Applied Genetics.	78, 79, 80, 81, 82	75, 76, 77, 78, 79	□/10	
Topic: Living Things—Classification							
✓	✓	✓	1 Identify five kingdoms of organisms and characteristics of each. • Describe the major characteristics of the five kingdoms. • Explain how living organisms can be classified according to similarities in structure, behavior, food needs, and chemical makeup into kingdoms, phyla, classes, orders, families, genera, and species.	83, 84, 85, 86, 87, 88	51, 52, 53, 54, 55, 56	□/12	

LIFE SCIENCE

TESTS			Life Science Objectives (continued)	Question Numbers Test A	Question Numbers Test B	Number Correct	Proficient? Yes or No
SAT9	ITBS	Terra-Nova					

Topic: Living Things—Monerans, Protists, and Fungi

SAT9	ITBS	Terra-Nova	Objective	Test A	Test B	Number Correct	Proficient?
✓	✓		1 Identify the characteristics and structure of monerans, protists, and fungi. • List the harmful and beneficial effects of the organisms in these three kingdoms.	89, 90, 91, 93, 94, 95	57, 58, 59, 60, 61, 62, 63	□/13	

Topic: Living Things—Plants

✓	✓		1 Identify the characteristics and structure of nonvascular plants.	96, 97, 98	72, 73, 74	□/6	
✓	✓		2 Identify the characteristics and structure of vascular plants.	99, 100, 101, 102, 103	134, 135, 136, 137, 138	□/10	
	✓		3 Describe and compare various life processes of plants: life cycles, photosynthesis, cellular respiration, growth, and response to environmental stimuli.	104, 105, 106, 107, 108, 109, 110	127, 128, 129, 130, 131, 132, 133	□/14	

Topic: Living Things—Animals

✓	✓		1 Describe the characteristics of invertebrate animals. • Sort and classify invertebrates into groups according to life conditions, methods of obtaining food, life cycles, and behavior.	111, 112, 113, 114, 115, 116	139, 140, 141, 142, 143, 144	□/12	
✓	✓		2 Describe the characteristics of vertebrates. • Identify classes of vertebrates based on life conditions, methods of obtaining food, life cycles, and behavior.	117, 118, 119, 120, 121, 122	109, 110, 111, 112, 113, 114	□/12	

Topic: Living Things/Interdependence of Life

✓	✓	✓	1 Describe the characteristics of major biomes. • Describe the location of major biomes. • Describe the organisms found within biomes.	123, 124, 125, 126, 127	122, 123, 124, 125, 126	□/10	
✓	✓		2 Identify the relationship between organisms and the environment. • Identify components of an ecosystem. • Describe the role of organisms in an ecosystem. • Describe how energy moves through an ecosystem in food chains and food webs. • Observe and describe the role of ecological succession in ecosystems.	128, 129, 130, 131, 132, 133, 134, 135, 136, 137	99, 100, 101, 102, 103, 104, 105, 106, 107, 108	□/20	

Name _____ Date _____ Class _____

TESTS			Life Science Objectives *(continued)*	Question Numbers Test A	Question Numbers Test B	Number Correct	Proficient? Yes or No
SAT9	ITBS	TerraNova					
✓	✓	✓	3 Understand that organisms respond and adapt to their environments. • Identify components of an ecosystem to which organisms may respond. • Define and give examples of adaptation for survival of the species. • Analyze how natural or human events may have contributed to the extinction of some species.	138, 139, 140, 141, 142, 143, 144	115, 116, 117, 118, 119, 120, 121	$\frac{\Box}{14}$	

COMMENTS:

_____
Parent or Guardian Signature

Earth Science Diagnostic Test A

1. C	**26.** G	**51.** B	**76.** G	**101.** A	**126.** J
2. G	**27.** A	**52.** G	**77.** C	**102.** H	**127.** D
3. D	**28.** H	**53.** C	**78.** G	**103.** D	**128.** H
4. J	**29.** A	**54.** J	**79.** B	**104.** H	**129.** B
5. A	**30.** G	**55.** A	**80.** F	**105.** C	**130.** J
6. F	**31.** C	**56.** F	**81.** C	**106.** J	**131.** A
7. C	**32.** H	**57.** C	**82.** G	**107.** D	**132.** F
8. G	**33.** A	**58.** H	**83.** D	**108.** J	**133.** A
9. C	**34.** J	**59.** C	**84.** G	**109.** C	**134.** F
10. J	**35.** B	**60.** J	**85.** A	**110.** H	**135.** C
11. B	**36.** F	**61.** C	**86.** G	**111.** C	**136.** F
12. G	**37.** A	**62.** H	**87.** C	**112.** F	**137.** A
13. B	**38.** F	**63.** C	**88.** H	**113.** C	**138.** J
14. J	**39.** C	**64.** G	**89.** A	**114.** G	**139.** C
15. A	**40.** F	**65.** B	**90.** H	**115.** A	**140.** G
16. H	**41.** C	**66.** F	**91.** B	**116.** F	**141.** B
17. C	**42.** G	**67.** D	**92.** J	**117.** B	**142.** J
18. F	**43.** C	**68.** H	**93.** B	**118.** J	**143.** B
19. D	**44.** J	**69.** B	**94.** J	**119.** B	**144.** H
20. G	**45.** A	**70.** F	**95.** B	**120.** J	
21. A	**46.** H	**71.** A	**96.** H	**121.** D	
22. G	**47.** D	**72.** F	**97.** C	**122.** G	
23. B	**48.** F	**73.** A	**98.** J	**123.** C	
24. H	**49.** B	**74.** G	**99.** B	**124.** J	
25. C	**50.** F	**75.** C	**100.** J	**125.** B	

Earth Science Diagnostic Test B

1. A	26. F	51. A	76. F	101. D	126. H
2. G	27. C	52. F	77. A	102. J	127. A
3. C	28. H	53. B	78. H	103. A	128. F
4. H	29. C	54. H	79. C	104. J	129. D
5. B	30. J	55. C	80. J	105. C	130. J
6. H	31. B	56. J	81. B	106. G	131. A
7. C	32. F	57. C	82. H	107. C	132. G
8. F	33. D	58. G	83. C	108. H	133. D
9. B	34. G	59. A	84. G	109. C	134. F
10. H	35. A	60. H	85. C	110. H	135. B
11. C	36. J	61. C	86. J	111. D	136. G
12. J	37. C	62. G	87. A	112. H	137. D
13. B	38. J	63. D	88. G	113. D	138. F
14. F	39. B	64. F	89. B	114. F	139. D
15. B	40. G	65. C	90. J	115. C	140. H
16. G	41. C	66. H	91. B	116. J	141. A
17. B	42. J	67. B	92. F	117. D	142. H
18. F	43. C	68. G	93. B	118. G	143. B
19. C	44. G	69. B	94. J	119. D	144. G
20. F	45. A	70. H	95. B	120. J	
21. A	46. H	71. C	96. H	121. B	
22. F	47. A	72. F	97. B	122. H	
23. A	48. F	73. B	98. H	123. C	
24. J	49. A	74. G	99. D	124. F	
25. A	50. G	75. D	100. G	125. A	

ANSWER KEY

DIAGNOSTIC REPORT   EARTH SCIENCE

TESTS			Earth Science Objectives	Question Numbers Test A	Question Numbers Test B	Number Correct	Proficient? Yes or No
SAT9	ITBS	TerraNova					
Topic: Scientific Inquiry/Processes							
✓	✓	✓	1 Understand the fundamental concepts of science inquiry.	1, 2, 3	29, 30, 31	□/6	
✓	✓		2 Demonstrate the ability to perform science inquiry.	4, 5, 6	23, 24, 25	□/6	
✓	✓		3 Use the process skills of science. • Draw a conclusion from data. • Evaluate graphs of experimental data.	7, 8, 9	9, 10, 11	□/6	
✓			4 Apply safety skills.	10, 11, 12	38, 39, 40	□/6	
✓			5 Understand, use, and convert SI units.	13, 14, 15	32, 33, 34	□/6	
Topic: History and Nature of Science							
		✓	1 Understand science as a human endeavor. • Understand the changing nature of scientific knowledge. • Understand the history of science.	16, 17, 18	26, 27, 28	□/10	
Topic: Earth's Water							
✓			1 Describe the water cycle. • Identify parts of the water cycle. • Describe the distribution of fresh water and salt water on Earth.	19, 20, 21, 22, 23	12, 13, 14, 15, 16	□/16	
✓			2 Describe the characteristics of Earth's oceans. • Recognize the chemical and physical properties of ocean water. • Discuss the movements of ocean water in currents, tides, and waves. • Interpret a profile of the ocean floor.	24, 25, 26, 27, 28, 29, 30, 31	1, 2, 3, 4, 5, 6, 7, 8	□/6	

Name _____ Date _____ Class _____

EARTH SCIENCE

TESTS			Earth Science Objectives *(continued)*	Question Numbers Test A	Question Numbers Test B	Number Correct	Proficient? Yes or No
SAT9	ITBS	TerraNova					
Topic: Weather and Climate							
✓			1 Describe the composition and structure of Earth's atmosphere. • Identify the layers of Earth's atmosphere. • Describe the importance of the layers of Earth's atmosphere. • List the most abundant gases in Earth's atmosphere.	35, 36, 37, 38, 39, 40	17, 18, 19, 20, 21, 22	□/12	
✓		✓	2 Describe the factors that interact to cause weather, including air pressure, heat energy, winds, and moisture. • Compare different types of air masses and their effect on weather. • Analyze a graph about atmospheric conditions. • Interpret a diagram about atmospheric conditions.	41, 42, 43, 44, 45, 46	41, 42, 43, 44, 45, 46	□/12	
✓			3 Recognize and investigate weather phenomena. • Read and interpret a weather map. • Make a forecast based on a weather map.	47, 48, 49	86, 87, 88	□/6	
✓			4 Recognize Earth's major climate zones. • Identify factors that determine climate. • Differentiate among Earth's climate zones. • Give an example of a microclimate.	50, 51, 52, 53, 54, 55	73, 74, 75, 76, 77, 78	□/12	
Topic: Geology							
✓			1 Identify minerals by physical properties. • Uses properties such as hardness, shape, color, luster, streak, cleavage, and fracture to identify minerals.	56, 57, 58	70, 71, 72	□/6	
✓			2 Describe Earth's lithosphere. • Describe the structure of Earth's interior. • Identify rocks based on origins. • Interpret the rock cycle.	59, 60, 61, 62, 63, 64, 65	79, 80, 81, 82, 83, 84, 85	□/14	

EARTH SCIENCE

| TESTS | | | Earth Science Objectives (*continued*) | Question Numbers Test A | Question Numbers Test B | Number Correct | Proficient? Yes or No |
SAT9	ITBS	TerraNova					
✓	✓		3 Recognize that constructive and destructive forces change Earth's surface. • Explain the processes of weathering, erosion, and deposition • Understand the importance of soils and how they form. • Identify and explain the formation of structural features including mountains, plains, and plateaus. • Describe the formation of a river system.	66, 67, 68, 69, 70, 71, 72, 73, 74, 75	47, 48, 49, 50, 51, 52, 53, 54, 55, 56	□/20	
✓	✓	✓	4 Trace the scientific development of the idea of continental drift and the resulting plate tectonics theory. • Apply the theory of plate tectonics to explain plate movement and interactions. • Use diagrams to locate likely areas of volcanic and earthquake activity.	76, 77, 78, 79, 80, 81	64, 65, 66, 67, 68, 69	□/12	
✓			5 Use maps to interpret Earth's surface. • Interpret a topographic map. • Identify locations on maps and globes using a latitude/longitude coordinate system.	82, 83, 84, 85, 86	89, 90, 91, 92, 93	□/10	
✓			6 Describe Earth's history. • Describe major eras of geologic time. • Interpret geologic diagrams based on the principle of superposition. • Distinguish between relative and absolute dating. • Interpret a graph showing the rate of decay of elements.	87, 88, 89, 90, 91, 92, 93	57, 58, 59, 60, 61, 62, 63	□/14	
Topic: Human Interactions With the Environment							
✓		✓	1 Recognize that humans affect the environment. • Identify ways people cause pollution of water, air, and land. • Recognize the effects of pollution. • Discuss ways humans can correct pollution of water, air, and land.	94, 95, 96, 97, 98, 99, 100	117, 118, 119, 120, 121, 122, 123	□/14	

Name _____ Date _____ Class _____

© Pearson Education, Inc., publishing as Pearson Prentice Hall. All rights reserved.

TESTS			Earth Science Objectives *(continued)*	Question Numbers Test A	Question Numbers Test B	Number Correct	Proficient? Yes or No
SAT9	ITBS	TerraNova					
✓	✓	✓	2 Make inferences and draw conclusions about effects of human activity on Earth's resources. • Classify resources as renewable or nonrenewable. • Describe the use of alternative energy resources. • Define the terms *reduce, reuse,* and *recycle.*	101, 102, 103, 104, 105, 106, 107	110, 111, 112, 113, 114, 115, 116	□/14	✓

Topic: Earth in Space/Astronomy

TESTS			Earth Science Objectives	Question Numbers Test A	Question Numbers Test B	Number Correct	Proficient? Yes or No
SAT9	ITBS	TerraNova					
✓	✓		1 Identify patterns caused by interactions of Earth and the sun. • Explain the causes of the day/night cycle. • Use observations to make a prediction about time.	108, 109, 110, 111, 112, 113, 114	103, 104, 105, 106, 107, 108, 109	□/14	
✓	✓		2 Relate the movement of Earth, the moon, and the sun to patterns seen on Earth. • Relate movements of Earth and the moon to the observed cyclical phases of the moon. • Relate movements of Earth, the moon, and the sun to eclipses. • Relate movements of Earth, the moon, and the sun to tides.	115, 116, 117, 118, 119, 120	130, 131, 132, 133, 134, 135	□/12	
✓			3 Compare and contrast the objects in our solar system. • Associate orbits with the forces causing them. • Analyze a chart of planet characteristics. • Describe other objects (comets, asteroids) that make up our solar system.	121, 122, 123, 124, 125, 126	97, 98, 99, 100, 101, 102	□/12	

EARTH SCIENCE

Diagnostic Report   **193**

EARTH SCIENCE

TESTS			Earth Science Objectives *(continued)*	Question Numbers Test A	Question Numbers Test B	Number Correct	Proficient? Yes or No
SAT9	ITBS	TerraNova					
		✓	4 Understand that Earth is part of the universe. • Describe scientific evidence for the origin and evolution of the universe. • Explain the use of the speed of light to measure distances in the universe. • Describe how galaxies differ.	127, 128, 129, 130, 131, 132	136, 137, 138, 139, 140, 141	□/12	
✓	✓		5 Understand that stars have life cycles. • Explain the general life cycle of a star, including formation, transitions, and death. • Interpret a Hertzsprung-Russell Diagram.	133, 134, 135, 136, 137, 138	124, 125, 126, 127, 128, 129	□/12	
		✓	6 Describe technology used to explore and monitor outer space,	139, 140,	142, 143,	□/6	
		✓	including probes, rockets, telescopes, and spectroscopes. 7 Recognize the impact of space exploration on society.	141 142, 143, 144	144 94, 95, 96	□/6	

COMMENTS:

Parent or Guardian Signature _____

Physical Science Diagnostic Test A

1. C	**26.** H	**51.** C	**76.** J	**101.** B	**126.** F
2. J	**27.** D	**52.** H	**77.** A	**102.** J	**127.** A
3. C	**28.** H	**53.** D	**78.** H	**103.** B	**128.** H
4. J	**29.** B	**54.** F	**79.** C	**104.** J	**129.** C
5. B	**30.** G	**55.** D	**80.** J	**105.** D	**130.** F
6. H	**31.** C	**56.** F	**81.** B	**106.** G	**131.** B
7. D	**32.** F	**57.** C	**82.** F	**107.** A	**132.** F
8. J	**33.** C	**58.** J	**83.** A	**108.** F	**133.** A
9. A	**34.** J	**59.** C	**84.** G	**109.** C	**134.** G
10. F	**35.** B	**60.** H	**85.** A	**110.** G	**135.** B
11. C	**36.** H	**61.** B	**86.** J	**111.** A	**136.** F
12. G	**37.** B	**62.** J	**87.** D	**112.** J	**137.** A
13. D	**38.** H	**63.** D	**88.** H	**113.** B	**138.** H
14. H	**39.** A	**64.** F	**89.** C	**114.** G	**139.** C
15. B	**40.** G	**65.** B	**90.** F	**115.** C	**140.** G
16. F	**41.** B	**66.** G	**91.** C	**116.** J	
17. C	**42.** J	**67.** C	**92.** H	**117.** C	
18. H	**43.** C	**68.** H	**93.** C	**118.** F	
19. B	**44.** H	**69.** B	**94.** G	**119.** D	
20. F	**45.** C	**70.** H	**95.** A	**120.** G	
21. B	**46.** F	**71.** D	**96.** H	**121.** A	
22. G	**47.** A	**72.** G	**97.** C	**122.** G	
23. C	**48.** F	**73.** C	**98.** G	**123.** C	
24. G	**49.** B	**74.** J	**99.** B	**124.** H	
25. D	**50.** J	**75.** B	**100.** G	**125.** A	

ANSWER KEY

Physical Science Diagnostic Test B

1. B	26. H	51. C	76. J	101. A	126. G
2. J	27. A	52. J	77. B	102. H	127. C
3. B	28. F	53. B	78. H	103. B	128. H
4. G	29. D	54. F	79. C	104. F	129. C
5. C	30. H	55. D	80. H	105. A	130. G
6. G	31. C	56. J	81. B	106. G	131. A
7. A	32. J	57. D	82. G	107. C	132. J
8. G	33. D	58. J	83. A	108. F	133. D
9. B	34. H	59. B	84. F	109. B	134. G
10. H	35. A	60. H	85. D	110. J	135. A
11. D	36. H	61. D	86. J	111. A	136. G
12. G	37. D	62. F	87. B	112. H	137. B
13. C	38. H	63. C	88. H	113. B	138. F
14. H	39. B	64. F	89. C	114. J	139. C
15. C	40. H	65. D	90. J	115. B	140. H
16. G	41. D	66. H	91. C	116. H	
17. C	42. J	67. B	92. G	117. A	
18. G	43. C	68. G	93. A	118. H	
19. C	44. H	69. A	94. H	119. C	
20. F	45. A	70. F	95. A	120. F	
21. B	46. H	71. A	96. G	121. D	
22. J	47. C	72. F	97. A	122. J	
23. C	48. F	73. C	98. G	123. B	
24. G	49. A	74. G	99. C	124. G	
25. B	50. H	75. D	100. F	125. B	

Name _____ Date _____ Class _____

DIAGNOSTIC REPORT   PHYSICAL SCIENCE

TESTS SAT9	ITBS	TerraNova	Physical Science Objectives	Question Numbers Test A	Question Numbers Test B	Number Correct	Proficient? Yes or No
Topic: Scientific Inquiry/Process							
✓		✓	1 Understand the fundamental concepts of science inquiry.	1, 2, 3, 4	30, 31, 32, 33	□/8	
✓	✓		2 Demonstrate the ability to perform science inquiry. • Associate a scientific instrument with its use.	5, 6, 7	37, 38, 39	□/6	
✓	✓		3 Use the process skills of science. • Draw a conclusion from data. • Evaluate graphs of experimental data. • Read a measure of mass.	8, 9, 10, 11, 12	25, 26, 27, 28, 29	□/10	
	✓		4 Apply safety skills.	13, 14, 15	10, 11, 12	□/6	
	✓		5 Understand, use, and convert SI units.	16, 17, 18	43, 44, 45	□/6	
Topic: Science and Technology							
✓		✓	1 Analyze technological design. • Natural/synthetic. • Abilities of technological design. • Understanding science/technology.	19, 20, 21	7, 8, 9	□/6	
Topic: Forces and Motion							
✓		✓	1 Read a graph about motion. • Interpret a graph about the motion of an object. • Extrapolate data from a graph about the motion of an object. • Analyze a graph to make a prediction about motion.	22, 23, 24	16, 17, 18	□/6	
✓		✓	2 Draw a conclusion based on experimental data about motion • Use a chart to make a prediction about motion.	25, 26, 27	40, 41, 42	□/6	
✓		✓	3 Understand the relationships among speed, time, distance, velocity, and acceleration. • Perform calculations involving speed, time, and distance. • Compare and contrast speed, velocity, and acceleration.	28, 29, 30	4, 5, 6	□/6	
✓		✓	4 Analyze Newton's laws of motion. • Make a prediction about the effect of force on an object. • Predict the relative effect of variables on force experiment.	31, 32, 33	34, 35, 36	□/6	

PHYSICAL SCIENCE

PHYSICAL SCIENCE

| TESTS | | | Physical Science Objectives *(continued)* | Question Numbers Test A | Question Numbers Test B | Number Correct | Proficient? Yes or No |
SAT9	ITBS	TerraNova					
	✓	✓	**5** Examine forces in nature. • Analyze gravity. • Analyze friction. • Identify electromagnetic forces.	34, 35, 36	22, 23, 24	□/6	
✓	✓	✓	**6** Define momentum and the law of the conservation of momentum.	37, 38, 39	19, 20, 21	□/6	
✓	✓		**7** Understand the relationship between force and pressure • Make a prediction about pressure.	40, 41, 42	1, 2, 3	□/6	
✓	✓		**8** Analyze forces in fluids.	43, 44, 45	13, 14, 15	6/6	
Topic: Mechanics							
✓	✓	✓	**1** Identify simple machines. • Draw a conclusion about simple machines. • Deduce the relative amounts of energy used in a simple machine.	46, 47, 48	70, 71, 72	□/6	
✓	✓		**2** Define work and power	49, 50, 51	73, 74, 75	□/6	
Topic: Energy and its Transformations							
✓	✓	✓	**1** Apply an understanding of energy changes—energy transfer, energy transformations, and conservation of energy. • Sequence changes in energy. • Apply an understanding of energy transfer. • Evaluate models of energy transfer.	52, 53, 54, 55, 56, 57	61, 62, 63, 64, 65, 66	□/12	
✓	✓		**2** Analyze the transfer of energy through waves.	58, 59, 60	88, 89, 90	□/6	
✓	✓		**3** Describe mechanical energy. • Associate a situation with an energy concept.	61, 62, 63	85, 86, 87	□/6	
✓	✓		**4** Apply an understanding of light waves as part of the electromagnetic spectrum.	64, 65, 66	67, 68, 69	□/6	
✓	✓		**5** Analyze the transmission of light. • Associate cause/effect of light transmission. • Use a model of light to make a prediction. • Make a prediction about light transmission.	67, 68, 69	79, 80, 81	□/6	

Name _____ Date _____ Class _____

PHYSICAL SCIENCE

TESTS SAT9	ITBS	TerraNova	Physical Science Objectives *(continued)*	Question Numbers Test A	Question Numbers Test B	Number Correct	Proficient? Yes or No
✓	✓	✓	6 Recognize ways light interacts with objects: reflection, refraction, absorption.	70, 71, 72	76, 77, 78	□/6	
	✓	✓	7 Analyze the phenomenon of color.	73, 74, 75, 76	57, 58, 59, 60	□/8	
✓	✓	✓	8 Examine heat and thermal energy. • Predict the effects of heat on objects. • Use observation to determine the relative amount of energy in a substance.	77, 78, 79, 80	49, 50, 51, 52	□/8	
	✓	✓	9 Describe the transfer of thermal energy.	81, 82, 83	82, 83, 84	□/6	
	✓	✓	10 Explain static electricity.	84, 85, 86, 87	53, 54, 55, 56	□/8	
	✓	✓	11 Analyze electrical circuits.	88, 89, 90	46, 47, 48	□/6	
	✓	✓	12 Understand magnetism.	91, 92, 93, 94	126, 127, 128, 129	□/8	
	✓	✓	13 Explain the interaction between magnetism and electricity.	95, 96, 97, 98, 99	136, 137, 138, 139, 140	□/10	
✓	✓	✓	14 Describe how sound is produced and transmitted • Evaluate models of sound.	100, 101, 102, 103, 104	121, 122, 123, 124, 125	□/10	
✓	✓	✓	15 Discuss the characteristics of sound: pitch and loudness.	105, 106, 107	133, 134, 135	□/6	

Topic: Characteristics of Matter

TESTS SAT9	ITBS	TerraNova	Physical Science Objectives	Question Numbers Test A	Question Numbers Test B	Number Correct	Proficient? Yes or No
✓	✓	✓	1 Interpret data about the physical properties of matter. • Analyze a chart about the physical properties of matter. • Draw a conclusion about physical properties of matter. • Use data to predict the physical properties of matter.	108, 109, 110	111, 112, 113	□/6	
✓	✓	✓	2 Analyze physical changes in matter. • Apply an understanding of changes in states of matter. • Identify the cause of a physical change. • Apply an understanding of motion in molecules.	111, 112, 113	130, 131, 132	□/6	
	✓	✓	3 Explain the structure of atoms.	114, 115, 116	114, 115, 116	□/6	
	✓	✓	4 Analyze chemical building blocks.	117, 118, 119, 120	107, 108, 109, 110	□/8	
	✓	✓	5 Analyze the periodic table of the elements. • Understand the organization of the periodic table.	121, 122, 123, 124, 125, 126	97, 98, 99, 100, 101, 102	□/12	

PHYSICAL SC

TESTS			Physical Science Objectives *(continued)*	Question Numbers Test A	Question Numbers Test B	Number Correct	Proficient? Yes or No
SAT9	ITBS	TerraNova					
	✓	✓	6 Identify factors that affect how materials react chemically. • Associate changes in substances with changes in energy.	127, 128, 129, 130	117, 118, 119, 120	□/8	
	✓	✓	7 Analyze the conservation of mass in a chemical reaction	131, 132, 133, 134	103, 104, 105, 106	□/8	
	✓	✓	8 Identify acids and bases and the reactions between them.	135, 136, 137, 138, 139, 140	91, 92, 93, 94, 95, 96	□/12	

COMMENTS:

_____

Parent or Guardian Signature

TEST ANSWER SHEET

1 Ⓐ Ⓑ Ⓒ Ⓓ	31 Ⓐ Ⓑ Ⓒ Ⓓ	61 Ⓐ Ⓑ Ⓒ Ⓓ	91 Ⓐ Ⓑ Ⓒ Ⓓ	121 Ⓐ Ⓑ Ⓒ Ⓓ
2 Ⓕ Ⓖ Ⓗ Ⓙ	32 Ⓕ Ⓖ Ⓗ Ⓙ	62 Ⓕ Ⓖ Ⓗ Ⓙ	92 Ⓕ Ⓖ Ⓗ Ⓙ	122 Ⓕ Ⓖ Ⓗ Ⓙ
3 Ⓐ Ⓑ Ⓒ Ⓓ	33 Ⓐ Ⓑ Ⓒ Ⓓ	63 Ⓐ Ⓑ Ⓒ Ⓓ	93 Ⓐ Ⓑ Ⓒ Ⓓ	123 Ⓐ Ⓑ Ⓒ Ⓓ
4 Ⓕ Ⓖ Ⓗ Ⓙ	34 Ⓕ Ⓖ Ⓗ Ⓙ	64 Ⓕ Ⓖ Ⓗ Ⓙ	94 Ⓕ Ⓖ Ⓗ Ⓙ	124 Ⓕ Ⓖ Ⓗ Ⓙ
5 Ⓐ Ⓑ Ⓒ Ⓓ	35 Ⓐ Ⓑ Ⓒ Ⓓ	65 Ⓐ Ⓑ Ⓒ Ⓓ	95 Ⓐ Ⓑ Ⓒ Ⓓ	125 Ⓐ Ⓑ Ⓒ Ⓓ
6 Ⓕ Ⓖ Ⓗ Ⓙ	36 Ⓕ Ⓖ Ⓗ Ⓙ	66 Ⓕ Ⓖ Ⓗ Ⓙ	96 Ⓕ Ⓖ Ⓗ Ⓙ	126 Ⓕ Ⓖ Ⓗ Ⓙ
7 Ⓐ Ⓑ Ⓒ Ⓓ	37 Ⓐ Ⓑ Ⓒ Ⓓ	67 Ⓐ Ⓑ Ⓒ Ⓓ	97 Ⓐ Ⓑ Ⓒ Ⓓ	127 Ⓐ Ⓑ Ⓒ Ⓓ
8 Ⓕ Ⓖ Ⓗ Ⓙ	38 Ⓕ Ⓖ Ⓗ Ⓙ	68 Ⓕ Ⓖ Ⓗ Ⓙ	98 Ⓕ Ⓖ Ⓗ Ⓙ	128 Ⓕ Ⓖ Ⓗ Ⓙ
9 Ⓐ Ⓑ Ⓒ Ⓓ	39 Ⓐ Ⓑ Ⓒ Ⓓ	69 Ⓐ Ⓑ Ⓒ Ⓓ	99 Ⓐ Ⓑ Ⓒ Ⓓ	129 Ⓐ Ⓑ Ⓒ Ⓓ
10 Ⓕ Ⓖ Ⓗ Ⓙ	40 Ⓕ Ⓖ Ⓗ Ⓙ	70 Ⓕ Ⓖ Ⓗ Ⓙ	100 Ⓕ Ⓖ Ⓗ Ⓙ	130 Ⓕ Ⓖ Ⓗ Ⓙ
11 Ⓐ Ⓑ Ⓒ Ⓓ	41 Ⓐ Ⓑ Ⓒ Ⓓ	71 Ⓐ Ⓑ Ⓒ Ⓓ	101 Ⓐ Ⓑ Ⓒ Ⓓ	131 Ⓐ Ⓑ Ⓒ Ⓓ
12 Ⓕ Ⓖ Ⓗ Ⓙ	42 Ⓕ Ⓖ Ⓗ Ⓙ	72 Ⓕ Ⓖ Ⓗ Ⓙ	102 Ⓕ Ⓖ Ⓗ Ⓙ	132 Ⓕ Ⓖ Ⓗ Ⓙ
13 Ⓐ Ⓑ Ⓒ Ⓓ	43 Ⓐ Ⓑ Ⓒ Ⓓ	73 Ⓐ Ⓑ Ⓒ Ⓓ	103 Ⓐ Ⓑ Ⓒ Ⓓ	133 Ⓐ Ⓑ Ⓒ Ⓓ
14 Ⓕ Ⓖ Ⓗ Ⓙ	44 Ⓕ Ⓖ Ⓗ Ⓙ	74 Ⓕ Ⓖ Ⓗ Ⓙ	104 Ⓕ Ⓖ Ⓗ Ⓙ	134 Ⓕ Ⓖ Ⓗ Ⓙ
15 Ⓐ Ⓑ Ⓒ Ⓓ	45 Ⓐ Ⓑ Ⓒ Ⓓ	75 Ⓐ Ⓑ Ⓒ Ⓓ	105 Ⓐ Ⓑ Ⓒ Ⓓ	135 Ⓐ Ⓑ Ⓒ Ⓓ
16 Ⓕ Ⓖ Ⓗ Ⓙ	46 Ⓕ Ⓖ Ⓗ Ⓙ	76 Ⓕ Ⓖ Ⓗ Ⓙ	106 Ⓕ Ⓖ Ⓗ Ⓙ	136 Ⓕ Ⓖ Ⓗ Ⓙ
17 Ⓐ Ⓑ Ⓒ Ⓓ	47 Ⓐ Ⓑ Ⓒ Ⓓ	77 Ⓐ Ⓑ Ⓒ Ⓓ	107 Ⓐ Ⓑ Ⓒ Ⓓ	137 Ⓐ Ⓑ Ⓒ Ⓓ
18 Ⓕ Ⓖ Ⓗ Ⓙ	48 Ⓕ Ⓖ Ⓗ Ⓙ	78 Ⓕ Ⓖ Ⓗ Ⓙ	108 Ⓕ Ⓖ Ⓗ Ⓙ	138 Ⓕ Ⓖ Ⓗ Ⓙ
19 Ⓐ Ⓑ Ⓒ Ⓓ	49 Ⓐ Ⓑ Ⓒ Ⓓ	79 Ⓐ Ⓑ Ⓒ Ⓓ	109 Ⓐ Ⓑ Ⓒ Ⓓ	139 Ⓐ Ⓑ Ⓒ Ⓓ
20 Ⓕ Ⓖ Ⓗ Ⓙ	50 Ⓕ Ⓖ Ⓗ Ⓙ	80 Ⓕ Ⓖ Ⓗ Ⓙ	110 Ⓕ Ⓖ Ⓗ Ⓙ	140 Ⓕ Ⓖ Ⓗ Ⓙ
21 Ⓐ Ⓑ Ⓒ Ⓓ	51 Ⓐ Ⓑ Ⓒ Ⓓ	81 Ⓐ Ⓑ Ⓒ Ⓓ	111 Ⓐ Ⓑ Ⓒ Ⓓ	141 Ⓐ Ⓑ Ⓒ Ⓓ
22 Ⓕ Ⓖ Ⓗ Ⓙ	52 Ⓕ Ⓖ Ⓗ Ⓙ	82 Ⓕ Ⓖ Ⓗ Ⓙ	112 Ⓕ Ⓖ Ⓗ Ⓙ	142 Ⓕ Ⓖ Ⓗ Ⓙ
23 Ⓐ Ⓑ Ⓒ Ⓓ	53 Ⓐ Ⓑ Ⓒ Ⓓ	83 Ⓐ Ⓑ Ⓒ Ⓓ	113 Ⓐ Ⓑ Ⓒ Ⓓ	143 Ⓐ Ⓑ Ⓒ Ⓓ
24 Ⓕ Ⓖ Ⓗ Ⓙ	54 Ⓕ Ⓖ Ⓗ Ⓙ	84 Ⓕ Ⓖ Ⓗ Ⓙ	114 Ⓕ Ⓖ Ⓗ Ⓙ	144 Ⓕ Ⓖ Ⓗ Ⓙ
25 Ⓐ Ⓑ Ⓒ Ⓓ	55 Ⓐ Ⓑ Ⓒ Ⓓ	85 Ⓐ Ⓑ Ⓒ Ⓓ	115 Ⓐ Ⓑ Ⓒ Ⓓ	145 Ⓐ Ⓑ Ⓒ Ⓓ
26 Ⓕ Ⓖ Ⓗ Ⓙ	56 Ⓕ Ⓖ Ⓗ Ⓙ	86 Ⓕ Ⓖ Ⓗ Ⓙ	116 Ⓕ Ⓖ Ⓗ Ⓙ	146 Ⓕ Ⓖ Ⓗ Ⓙ
27 Ⓐ Ⓑ Ⓒ Ⓓ	57 Ⓐ Ⓑ Ⓒ Ⓓ	87 Ⓐ Ⓑ Ⓒ Ⓓ	117 Ⓐ Ⓑ Ⓒ Ⓓ	147 Ⓐ Ⓑ Ⓒ Ⓓ
28 Ⓕ Ⓖ Ⓗ Ⓙ	58 Ⓕ Ⓖ Ⓗ Ⓙ	88 Ⓕ Ⓖ Ⓗ Ⓙ	118 Ⓕ Ⓖ Ⓗ Ⓙ	148 Ⓕ Ⓖ Ⓗ Ⓙ
29 Ⓐ Ⓑ Ⓒ Ⓓ	59 Ⓐ Ⓑ Ⓒ Ⓓ	89 Ⓐ Ⓑ Ⓒ Ⓓ	119 Ⓐ Ⓑ Ⓒ Ⓓ	149 Ⓐ Ⓑ Ⓒ Ⓓ
30 Ⓕ Ⓖ Ⓗ Ⓙ	60 Ⓕ Ⓖ Ⓗ Ⓙ	90 Ⓕ Ⓖ Ⓗ Ⓙ	120 Ⓕ Ⓖ Ⓗ Ⓙ	150 Ⓕ Ⓖ Ⓗ Ⓙ

STANDARDIZED TEST
PREPARATION WORKBOOK
ANSWER KEY AND CORRELATIONS

Correlation of Prentice Hall *Science Explorer Test Preparation Workbook* Grade 6 SAT9 Prep Practice Test to the SAT9 Content and Process Clusters

Stanford 9 Clusters: Intermediate 3	Test Questions
Content	
Earth and Space Science: Demonstrate an understanding of the structure of Earth, Earth's history, Earth in the solar system, natural hazards, and impacts of technology on Earth.	1, 6, 10, 12, 17, 22, 26, 29, 31, 33, 34, 35, 37
Physical Science: Demonstrate an understanding of properties and changes in matter, forces and motion, transfer of energy, and uses of physical concepts in technological design.	3, 8, 14, 15, 16, 18, 20, 24, 27, 30, 32, 34, 38, 40
Life Science: Demonstrate an understanding of the structure and function in living systems, organism behavior, ecosystems, diversity of organisms, health, and technological benefits and problems.	2, 4, 5, 7, 9, 11, 13, 19, 21, 23, 25, 28, 36, 39
Process	
Using Evidence and Models: Use and analyze evidence, science experiments, and models of the processes in the natural and technological worlds, including historical evidence and historically significant models.	2, 7, 13, 20, 22, 27, 30, 34, 35
Recognizing Constancy and Patterns of Change: Use observations, data, and basic understanding to recognize and analyze patterns in the natural and technological worlds.	11, 14, 18, 19, 22, 23, 24, 26, 27, 33, 34, 35, 38
Comparing Form and Function: Use observations, data, and basic understanding to compare form and functions of objects and organisms in the natural and technological worlds.	10, 18, 28, 34

Correlation of Prentice Hall *Science Explorer Test Preparation Workbook* Grade 6 ITBS Prep Practice Test to the Iowa Test of Basic Skills Objectives, Level 12

ITBS Standards, Level 12	Test Questions
1.0 Nature of Science	
1.1 Science inquiry methods	1, 9, 20, 34
1.2 Science process skills	5, 15, 25, 37
2.0 Life Science	
2.1 Life processes	2, 18
2.2 Characteristics of animals	14, 31
2.3 Characteristics of plants	6, 22
2.4 Body processes	26, 42
2.5 Continuity of life	29, 39
2.6 Environmental adaptation	24, 33
2.7 Environmental interactions	10, 16
3.0 Earth and Space Science	
3.1 Earth's surface	11, 19
3.2 Forces of nature	27, 41
3.3 Renewability of resources	13, 28
3.4 Atmosphere	3, 35
3.5 The universe	7, 21
4.0 Physical Science	
4.1 Forces	8, 40
4.2 Forms of energy	36, 38
4.3 Electricity	4, 17
4.4 Magnetism	23, 32
4.5 Characteristics of matter	12, 30

Correlation of Prentice Hall *Science Explorer Test Preparation Workbook* Grade 6 TerraNova Prep Practice Test to TerraNova Objectives, Level 16

TerraNova Objectives, Level 16	Test Questions
19 **Science Inquiry:** Demonstrate an understanding of the fundamental concepts of science inquiry. Demonstrate the ability to perform science inquiry.	2, 8, 12, 16, 20, 22, 26, 27, 32, 36
20 **Physical Science:** Demonstrate an understanding of the fundamental concepts and principles of physical science. Apply physical science knowledge to investigations and real-world contexts.	1, 9, 13, 18, 21, 23, 29, 33, 37, 39
21 **Life Science:** Demonstrate an understanding of the fundamental concepts and principles of life science. Apply life science knowledge to investigations and real-world contexts.	4, 6, 10, 14, 17, 24, 28, 30, 34, 38
22 **Earth and Space Science:** Demonstrate an understanding of the fundamental concepts and principles of Earth and space science. Apply Earth and space science knowledge to investigations and real-world contexts.	3, 5, 7, 11, 15, 19, 25, 31, 35, 40

Grade 6 SAT9 Prep Practice Test

1.	B		21.	B
2.	G		22.	G
3.	D		23.	B
4.	J		24.	H
5.	D		25.	D
6.	F		26.	G
7.	D		27.	A
8.	F		28.	J
9.	D		29.	A
10.	G		30.	J
11.	B		31.	A
12.	G		32.	F
13.	B		33.	B
14.	H		34.	F
15.	B		35.	A
16.	F		36.	F
17.	C		37.	D
18.	G		38.	G
19.	B		39.	C
20.	G		40.	G

Grade 6 ITBS Prep Practice Test

1.	C	22.	L
2.	K	23.	B
3.	C	24.	J
4.	J	25.	A
5.	C	26.	K
6.	M	27.	C
7.	B	28.	M
8.	K	29.	A
9.	D	30.	K
10.	K	31.	C
11.	A	32.	L
12.	J	33.	B
13.	A	34.	M
14.	J	35.	B
15.	B	36.	K
16.	K	37.	D
17.	D	38.	J
18.	L	39.	D
19.	A	40.	J
20.	L	41.	D
21.	D	42.	L

Grade 6 TerraNova Prep Practice Test

1.	D		21.	D
2.	J		22.	F
3.	C		23.	C
4.	H		24.	J
5.	D		25.	D
6.	F		26.	F
7.	C		27.	D
8.	H		28.	F
9.	C		29.	B
10.	F		30.	F
11.	A		31.	C
12.	G		32.	J
13.	A		33.	B
14.	G		34.	F
15.	A		35.	C
16.	G		36.	G
17.	C		37.	A
18.	G		38.	J
19.	B		39.	C
20.	J		40.	G

**Correlation of Prentice Hall *Science Explorer Test Preparation Workbook*
Grade 7 SAT9 Prep Practice Test to the SAT9 Content and Process Clusters**

Stanford 9 Clusters: Advanced 1	Test Questions
Content	
Earth and Space Science: Demonstrate an understanding of the structure of Earth, Earth's history, Earth in the solar system, natural hazards, and impacts of technology on Earth.	1, 4, 8, 11, 14, 17, 21, 24, 27, 28, 29, 31
Physical Science: Demonstrate an understanding of properties and changes in matter, forces and motion, transfer of energy, and uses of physical concepts in technological design.	2, 5, 9, 12, 15, 19, 22, 25, 30, 33, 35, 38, 40
Life Science: Demonstrate an understanding of the structure and function in living systems, organism behavior, ecosystems, diversity of organisms, health, and technological benefits and problems.	3, 6, 7, 10, 13, 16, 18, 20, 23, 26, 32, 34, 36, 37, 39
Process	
Using Evidence and Models: Use and analyze evidence, science experiments, and models of the processes in the natural and technological worlds, including historical evidence and historically significant models.	5, 6, 7, 9, 10, 16, 19, 20, 23, 24, 25, 26
Recognizing Constancy and Patterns of Change: Use observations, data, and basic understanding to recognize and analyze patterns in the natural and technological worlds.	1, 2, 3, 4, 8, 9, 12, 16, 19, 25, 28, 35, 38, 40
Comparing Form and Function: Use observations, data, and basic understanding to compare form and functions of objects and organisms in the natural and technological worlds.	13, 14, 15, 20, 27, 29, 33, 34, 36

Correlation of Prentice Hall *Science Explorer Test Preparation Workbook* Grade 7 ITBS Prep Practice Test to the Iowa Test of Basic Skills Objectives, Level 13

ITBS Standards, Level 13	Test Questions
1.0 Nature of Science	
1.1 Science inquiry methods	11, 19, 26, 32
1.2 Science process skills	2, 14, 21, 33
2.0 Life Science	
2.1 Life processes	1, 9
2.2 Characteristics of animals	4, 23
2.3 Characteristics of plants	12, 36
2.4 Body processes	27, 42
2.5 Continuity of life	16, 18
2.6 Environmental interactions	29, 39
3.0 Earth and Space Science	
3.1 Earth's surface	8, 31
3.2 Forces of nature	24, 38
3.3 Renewability of resources	6, 40
3.4 Atmosphere	13, 35
3.5 The universe	20, 25, 37
4.0 Physical Science	
4.1 Forces	7, 28
4.2 Mechanics	10, 22
4.3 Forms of energy	30, 34, 41
4.4 Electricity	5, 17
4.5 Characteristics of matter	3, 15

Correlation of Prentice Hall *Science Explorer Test Preparation Workbook* Grade 7 TerraNova Prep Practice Test to TerraNova Objectives, Level 17

TerraNova Objectives, Level 17	Test Questions
19 **Science Inquiry:** Demonstrate an understanding of the fundamental concepts of science inquiry. Demonstrate the ability to perform science inquiry.	3, 9, 13, 16, 18, 22, 25, 30, 32, 39
20 **Physical Science:** Demonstrate an understanding of the fundamental concepts and principles of physical science. Apply physical science knowledge to investigations and real-world contexts.	1, 4, 8, 12, 17, 21, 26, 31, 35, 38
21 **Life Science:** Demonstrate an understanding of the fundamental concepts and principles of life science. Apply life science knowledge to investigations and real-world contexts.	5, 7, 11, 15, 19, 24, 27, 29, 33, 36
22 **Earth and Space Science:** Demonstrate an understanding of the fundamental concepts and principles of Earth and space science. Apply Earth and space science knowledge to investigations and real-world contexts.	2, 6, 10, 14, 20, 23, 28, 34, 37, 40

Grade 7 SAT9 Prep Practice Test

1.	B		21.	A
2.	F		22.	H
3.	C		23.	A
4.	F		24.	H
5.	D		25.	A
6.	H		26.	F
7.	D		27.	A
8.	F		28.	F
9.	D		29.	C
10.	H		30.	F
11.	A		31.	B
12.	J		32.	F
13.	D		33.	A
14.	G		34.	G
15.	B		35.	A
16.	G		36.	G
17.	A		37.	A
18.	F		38.	J
19.	B		39.	C
20.	J		40.	G

Grade 7 ITBS Prep Practice Test

1.	A	22.	J
2.	M	23.	C
3.	B	24.	L
4.	K	25.	D
5.	B	26.	K
6.	L	27.	C
7.	C	28.	K
8.	M	29.	A
9.	B	30.	K
10.	J	31.	C
11.	A	32.	M
12.	M	33.	A
13.	A	34.	M
14.	K	35.	A
15.	C	36.	K
16.	J	37.	C
17.	B	38.	L
18.	M	39.	A
19.	D	40.	L
20.	K	41.	C
21.	B	42.	K

Grade 7 TerraNova Prep Practice Test

1.	A	21.	B
2.	H	22.	J
3.	C	23.	C
4.	F	24.	G
5.	A	25.	A
6.	J	26.	H
7.	A	27.	B
8.	H	28.	F
9.	A	29.	B
10.	J	30.	F
11.	C	31.	D
12.	J	32.	H
13.	D	33.	C
14.	J	34.	J
15.	B	35.	B
16.	J	36.	H
17.	A	37.	A
18.	J	38.	H
19.	B	39.	D
20.	H	40.	F

Correlation of Prentice Hall *Science Explorer Test Preparation Workbook* Grade 8 SAT9 Prep Practice Test to the SAT9 Content and Process Clusters

Stanford 9 Clusters: Advanced 2	Test Questions
Content	
Earth and Space Science: Demonstrate an understanding of the structure of Earth, Earth's history, Earth in the solar system, natural hazards, and impacts of technology on Earth.	1, 3, 9, 10, 15, 18, 22, 26, 29, 32, 35, 37
Physical Science: Demonstrate an understanding of properties and changes in matter, forces and motion, transfer of energy, and uses of physical concepts in technological design.	2, 7, 8, 11, 12, 14, 16, 19, 23, 24, 25, 27, 30, 33, 35, 38, 39
Life Science: Demonstrate an understanding of the structure and function in living systems, organism behavior, ecosystems, diversity of organisms, health, and technological benefits and problems.	4, 5, 6, 13, 17, 20, 21, 28, 31, 34, 36, 40
Process	
Using Evidence and Models: Use and analyze evidence, science experiments, and models of the processes in the natural and technological worlds, including historical evidence and historically significant models.	7, 8, 9, 10, 16, 18, 20, 21, 27, 34, 37, 39
Recognizing Constancy and Patterns of Change: Use observations, data, and basic understanding to recognize and analyze patterns in the natural and technological worlds.	2, 4, 5, 6, 9, 10, 14, 15, 16, 26, 27, 29, 30, 36, 38, 40
Comparing Form and Function: Use observations, data, and basic understanding to compare form and functions of objects and organisms in the natural and technological worlds.	16, 19, 24, 28, 31, 33

**Correlation of Prentice Hall *Science Explorer Test Preparation Workbook*
Grade 8 ITBS Prep Practice Test to the Iowa Test of Basic Skills
Objectives, Level 14**

ITBS Standards, Level 14	Test Questions
1.0 Nature of Science	
1.1 Science inquiry methods	7, 14, 26, 27
1.2 Science process skills	4, 18, 33, 40
2.0 Life Science	
2.1 Life processes	13, 37
2.2 Characteristics of plants	3, 20
2.3 Body processes	11
2.4 Nutrition	16, 41
2.5 Continuity of life	6, 30
2.6 Environmental interactions	9, 23
2.7 Environmental adaptation	28
3.0 Earth and Space Science	
3.1 Earth's surface	17, 24
3.2 Forces of nature	1, 32
3.3 Renewability of resources	42
3.4 Atmosphere	5
3.5 Weather	22, 35
3.6 The universe	8, 39
4.0 Physical Science	
4.1 Mechanics	34, 38
4.2 Motion	2
4.3 Forces	15
4.4 Forms of energy	21
4.5 Electricity	25, 31
4.6 Characteristics of matter	36
4.7 Chemical reactions	12, 29
	10, 19